American Expansionism, 1783–1860

SEMINAR STUDIES IN HISTORY

American Expansionism, 1783–1860:

A Manifest Destiny?

MARK S. JOY

PEARSON

Longman

London • New York • Toronto • Sydney • Tokyo • Singapore
Hong Kong • Cape Town • Madrid • Paris • Amsterdam • Munich • Milan

PEARSON EDUCATION LIMITED

Head Office:
Edinburgh Gate
Harlow CM20 2JE
Tel: +44 (0)1279 623623
Fax: +44 (0)1279 431059

London Office:
128 Long Acre
London WC2E 9AN
Tel: +44 (0)20 7447 2000
Fax: +44 (0)20 7447 2170
Website: www.history-minds.com

First published in Great Britain in 2003

© Pearson Education Limited 2003

The right of Mark S. Joy to be identified as Author
of this Work has been asserted by him in accordance
with the Copyright, Designs and Patents Act 1988.

ISBN 0582 36965 7

British Library Cataloguing in Publication Data
A CIP catalogue record for this book can be obtained from the British Library

Library of Congress Cataloging in Publication Data
A CIP catalog record for this book can be obtained from the Library of Congress

10 9 8 7 6 5 4 3 2 1

Typeset by 7 in 10/12 Sabon Roman
Produced by Pearson Education Asia Pte Ltd.,
Printed in Malaysia, LSP
The Publishers' policy is to use paper manufactured from sustainable forests.

To Homer E. Socolofsky

CONTENTS

INTRODUCTION TO THE SERIES

Such is the pace of historical enquiry in the modern world that there is an ever-widening gap between the specialist article or monograph, incorporating the results of current research, and general surveys, which inevitably become out of date. *Seminar Studies in History* is designed to bridge this gap. The series was founded by Patrick Richardson in 1966 and his aim was to cover major themes in British, European and world history. Between 1980 and 1996 Roger Lockyer continued his work, before handing the editorship over to Clive Emsley and Gordon Martel. Clive Emsley is Professor of History at the Open University, while Gordon Martel is Professor of International History at the University of Northern British Columbia, Canada, and Senior Research Fellow at De Montfort University.

All the books are written by experts in their field who are not only familiar with the latest research but have often contributed to it. They are frequently revised, in order to take account of new information and interpretations. They provide a selection of documents to illustrate major themes and provoke discussion, and also a guide to further reading. The aim of *Seminar Studies in History* is to clarify complex issues without over-simplifying them, and to stimulate readers into deepening their knowledge and understanding of major themes and topics.

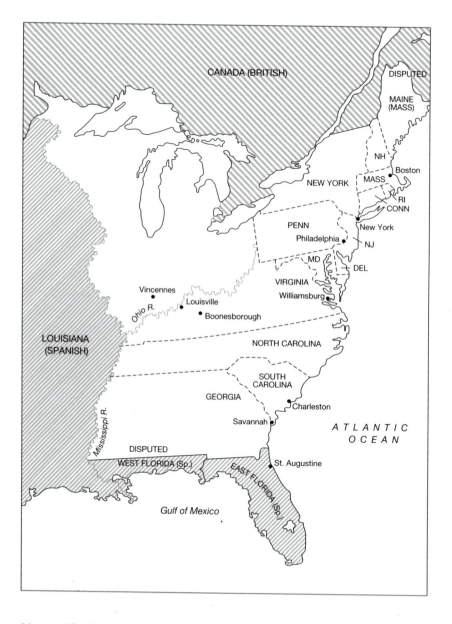

Map 1 The United States in 1783
Source: After Wexler, A. and Braun, M. (1995) *Atlas of Westward Expansion* (pub. New York: Facts on File), Map 1.9, p. 16

Map 2   Explorations of the Louisiana Purchase

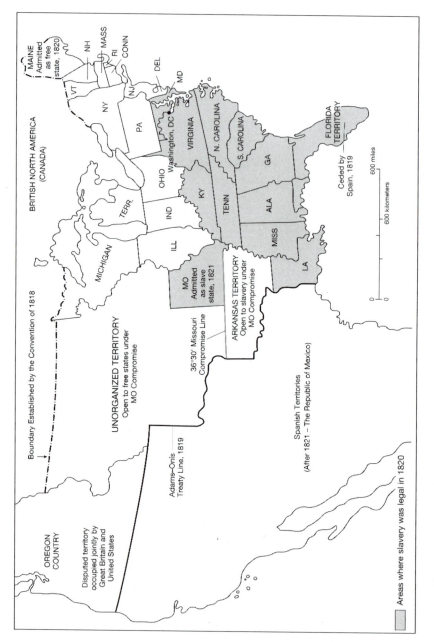

Map 3 The Convention of 1818, the Adams–Onís Treaty, and the Missouri Compromise

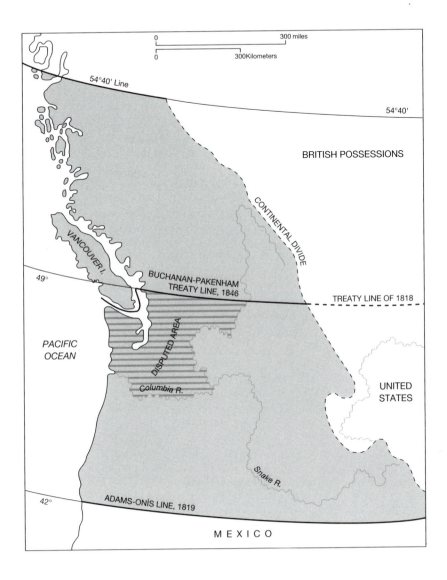

Map 4 The Oregon Dispute, 1818–1846

Map 5   The Mexican War, 1846–1848
Source: After Wexler, A. and Braun, M. (1995) *Atlas of Westward Expansion* (pub.
New York: Facts on File), Map 5.6, p. 107

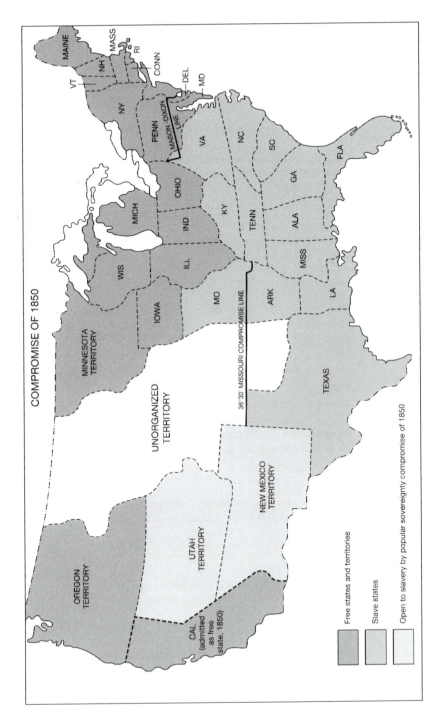

Map 6 The Compromise of 1850

CHRONOLOGY

1755

April
Skirmishes between French and British colonial forces in the forks of the Ohio River region mark the beginning of what becomes known as the French and Indian War; the North American conflict later becomes caught up in the Seven Years' War in Europe.

1756

15 May
Great Britain declares war on France, beginning the Seven Years' War in Europe.

1763

10 February
The Treaty of Paris ends the Seven Years' War and its American counterpart, the French and Indian War. France gives up most of its North American empire; Great Britain takes control of lands east of the Mississippi River, and east and west Florida.

May
Pontiac's Rebellion, an uprising of Indians on the western frontier, erupts in the British colonies.

7 October
King George III signs the Proclamation of 1763, setting up the Demarcation Line along the western frontier of the British North America colonies; settlement beyond this line is forbidden in an attempt to make peace with the Indians.

1775

19 April
Fighting commences between American colonists and British troops with skirmishes at Lexington and Concord, Massachusetts.

1776

4 July
The thirteen American colonies declare independence from Great Britain as the United States of America.

1777

15 November
The Continental Congress approves the Articles of Confederation as a frame of government for the US; Articles are submitted to the individual states for ratification, with unanimous approval required.

1778

Captain James Cook, sailing under the British flag, explores the Pacific Northwest coast of North America, which helps to establishes a British claim for the region.

1781

1 March | Upon ratification of Articles of Confederation by the final state (Maryland), Congress declares the document officially in force.

19 October | The surrender of Lord Cornwallis and his forces at Yorktown marks the end of British offensive actions in the American War of Independence.

1783

3 September | The Treaty of Paris is signed, marking the formal end of the American Revolution. Great Britain agrees to generous boundaries for the new American nation.

1785

8 May | Congress passes the Land Ordinance. Provides for a rectangular survey of lands west of the Ohio River, dividing the lands into 6-mile square townships. Land will be sold in minimum lots of 640 acres for $640.

1786

11–14 September | Delegates from five states attend a meeting in Annapolis, MD, to discuss problems with the Articles of Confederation. The delegates attending call for a national convention to address problems.

1787

25 May | Constitutional Convention begins meeting in Philadelphia, PA.

13 July | Congress passes the Northwest Ordinance, which details how lands in the Old Northwest would be organized for statehood. States thus created were to be equal to the original 13 states in all respects. Slavery was forbidden in this region.

17 September | The Constitution is signed by 39 delegates to the convention, and submitted to Congress.

28 September | Congress votes to submit the Constitution to the states for ratification. Approval by nine states is required.

1788

June and July | Although the Constitution has been ratified by the required nine states, most American leaders believe it will not work without the support of Virginia and New York. Virginia ratifies on 25 June and New York on 26 July.

1789

4 February	In the first presidential election under the Constitution, George Washington is elected first president of the United States; John Adams elected vice-president. Votes of the electors are not announced until 6 April.
4 March	The first Congress under the new Constitution assembles.

1790

28 October	Great Britain and Spain agree on the Nootka Sound Convention, in which Spain gives up claims to territory in the Oregon country. This strengthens Britain's claim to the region, but is disputed by the US.
September–October	A force of American militia is badly beaten in fighting with Indians near Ft Wayne in present-day Indiana; becomes known as Harmar's Humiliation, from the name of the US commander, Josiah Harmar.

1791

4 November	A large force of American troops are defeated by Indians in fighting near Ft Wayne in present-day Indiana. This becomes known St Clair's Shame, after the US commander, Arthur St Clair.

1792

Spring	Captain George Vancouver explores the Pacific Northwest, sailing under the British flag.
11 May	US Navy Captain Robert Gray sails the *Columbia* into what becomes known as Gray's Harbor and names the Columbia River after his ship.

1794

20 August	Battle of Fallen Timbers – The new American commander in the Old Northwest, General Anthony Wayne, defeats the Indians of the Northwest Confederacy in a battle along the Maumee River in present-day northwest Ohio.
19 November	John Jay concludes negotiations with Great Britain on a commercial treaty which becomes known as Jay's Treaty. Terms of the treaty are not made public in the United States until March 1795.

1795

24 June	After bitter debate, the US Senate ratifies the Jay Treaty.

3 August	General Anthony Wayne signs the Treaty of Greenville with 12 of the tribes of the Old Northwest region. The Indians cede large amounts of land and a boundary is set to separate white and Indian lands.
27 October	The Treaty of San Lorenzo, usually referred to in the US as Pinckney's Treaty, is signed by Thomas Pinckney, American Minister to Great Britain and special envoy to Spain. The treaty resolves some questions concerning the boundaries between US and Spanish territories, and grants American shippers the 'right of deposit' in New Orleans for three years.

1796

	The Cumberland Gap into eastern Kentucky is made passable to wagon traffic.
15 March	The Treaty of San Lorenzo or Pinckney's Treaty is ratified by the US Senate.

1800

10 May	Harrison's Land Law, also known as The Land Law of 1800, passed by Congress.
1 October	In the secret Treaty of San Ildefonso, Spain cedes control of Louisiana back to France.

1802

16 October	Spanish officials in Louisiana revoke the American 'right of deposit' in New Orleans.

1803

January	James Monroe sent to France to aid Robert Livingston in negotiating a purchase of New Orleans and West Florida.
30 April	James Monroe and Robert Livingston sign a draft treaty in France for the purchase of the Louisiana Territory.
31 August	The Corps of Discovery, or Lewis and Clark Expedition, sails down the Ohio to begin their exploration of the west. They will winter near St Louis on the Mississippi River before going up the Missouri River the following spring.
20 October	The US Senate ratifies the treaty for the Louisiana Purchase.
20 December	In a ceremony at New Orleans, the US takes formal possession of the Louisiana territory from French officials.

1804

14 May	The Lewis and Clark expedition leaves St Louis to travel up the Missouri River to explore the northwest.

| 27 October | Lewis and Clark expedition reaches the Mandan villages on the Missouri River near present-day Bismarck, ND. |

1805

7 April	The Lewis and Clark expedition leaves the Mandan villages to push on further into the northwest.
9 August	Lt Zebulon Pike is commissioned to explore the northern regions of the Louisiana Purchase, and specifically to attempt to discover the source of the Mississippi River.
November	The Lewis and Clark expedition reaches the Pacific Coast and makes preparations to winter there, near the site of present-day Astoria, Oregon.

1809

| July | The Shawnee Indian leader Tecumseh and his brother Tenskwatawa ('The Prophet') begin a campaign to confederate Indians in the Old Northwest region to resist further settlement in the region by whites. |

1810

| 26 September | Philemon Thomas leads a filibustering expedition into Spanish Florida, seizing the fort at Baton Rouge; settlers who join with him request annexation by the US. |
| 27 October | President Madison announces the annexation of portions of Spanish West Florida by the US. |

1811

| 7 November | William Henry Harrison, governor of the Indiana Territory, leads a 1000-man force in an attack on Prophetstown, the central settlement of Tecumseh's followers. Prophetstown is destroyed. |

1812

| June | President Madison asks Congress for a declaration of war against Great Britain, over maritime issues and British interference with American interests in the Old Northwest. The House approves a declaration of war on 4 June; the Senate follows on 18 June; on 19 June Madison formally declares that the US is at war. |

1813

| 5 October | American forces defeat the British and allied Indians at the Battle of the Thames in Ontario north of Lake Erie, the most important battle of the war in its effects on the northwest frontier. The Shawnee leader Tecumseh is killed in this battle. |

1814

7 November	Andrew Jackson captures Pensacola in Florida, as part of a plan to invade Spanish Florida.
24 December	American and British peace negotiators meeting in Ghent, Belgium, sign the Treaty of Ghent, ending the War of 1812.

1815

8 January	Unaware of the peace treaty signed the previous month, British and American forces fight a bitter battle at New Orleans. The British forces are repulsed in a battle that will make the American commander, Andrew Jackson, a national hero.

1817

28–29 April	Rush–Bagot Agreement concluded by the United States and Great Britain, to limit naval armaments on the Great Lakes. The agreement is unanimously approved by the US Senate on 16 April 1818, giving it the status of a treaty.

1818

20 October	In London, United States and British negotiators conclude the Convention of 1818, fixing the border between the United States and Canada from the Lake of the Woods westward to the continental divide. West of the Rocky Mountains, the 'Oregon Country' is left open to traders, settlers and maritime traffic of both nations.

1819

22 February	The Adams–Onís Treaty, or the Transcontinental Treaty, is signed. The treaty fixes the boundary between US and Spanish possessions, and Spain cedes East Florida to the United States, and renounces any claim to West Florida, which the US has already annexed.

1820

3 March	The US Congress approves the Missouri Compromise, admitting Missouri as a slave state and Maine as a free state. In the Louisiana Purchase lands, except for Missouri, slavery will be prohibited north of 36° 30'.

1821

24 February	Mexico declares independence from Spain.
24 August	Spain recognizes the independence of Mexico.

1822

19 May   Agustín de Iturbide seizes power in Mexico and declares himself
                Emperor.

1823

19 March   Iturbide abdicates as Emperor of Mexico; establishment of the
                Republic of Mexico.

2 December   President Monroe pronounces the 'Monroe Doctrine' in his
                annual message to Congress.

1827

6 August   The Treaty of Joint Occupation signed by negotiators from the
                US and Great Britain. The treaty provides for a continuation of
                the policy of 'joint occupation' in Oregon.

1830

28 May   President Andrew Jackson signs the Indian Removal Bill,
                providing for an exchange of lands west of the Mississippi River
                for the tribal lands of Indians living in the East.

1835–1842   When a faction within the Seminole tribe refuses to leave
                Florida peacefully, the US Army is sent in to force them out. The
                'Seminole War' rages for seven years, after which the army
                simply gives up, and a portion of the Seminole are allowed to
                remain in Florida.

1836

23 February–   The siege of the Alamo in San Antonio, by Mexican troops.
   6 March   The siege ends on 6 March with the death of all the
                defenders.

2 March   Settlers in Texas declare their independence from Mexico,
                beginning the Texas Revolution.

27 March   Approximately 300 Texan soldiers are massacred by Santa
                Anna's forces after surrendering at the Battle of Goliad.

21 April   The defeat and capture of Santa Anna by Texan forces at the
                Battle of San Jacinto marks the end of the fighting in the Texas
                Revolution.

September   Sam Houston elected as president of the Republic of Texas;
                voters in Texas in a referendum vote to seek annexation by the
                United States.

1837

3 March   The US grants official recognition to the Republic of Texas.

1841

4 September   The Distribution-Pre-Emption Act is passed by the US Congress. Settlers who have settled on public lands have the first right to purchase them when the lands officially become available for purchase.

1842

9 August   The Webster–Ashburton agreement between the United States and Great Britain is signed, settling disputes on the Canadian–Maine border region.

1844

8 June   A treaty for the annexation of Texas is rejected by the US Senate.

1845

25 January   The US House of Representatives approves the joint resolution for the annexation of Texas.

27 February   The US Senate approves the joint resolution for the annexation of Texas.

July   Citizens of Texas approve annexation by the US in a referendum.

1846

15 June   The Oregon Treaty ratified by the US Senate; provides for extending the US Canadian boundary westward along the 49th parallel.

1846

13 January   President Polk orders US troops to the Rio Grande area.

24 April   Outbreak of fighting between US and Mexican forces along the Rio Grande.

9 May   The report from Zachary Taylor concerning hostilities in the Rio Grande area reaches Polk.

13 May   The US Congress declares that a 'state of war' exists between the US and Mexico 'by the act of the Republic of Mexico ...'

8 May   Battle of Palo Alto in northern Mexico.

9 May   Battle of Resaca de la Palma in northern Mexico.

18 May	Taylor's forces occupy Matamoros, Mexico.
7 July	US naval forces under Commodore John D. Sloat capture Monterey in California.
8 August	The Wilmot Proviso, to bar slavery from any territory acquired from Mexico, introduced as an amendment to a war appropriations bill.
18 August	Stephen Kearny's forces occupy Santa Fé, the capital of New Mexico.
24 September	Taylor's forces capture Monterrey, Mexico.

1847

22–23 February	Battle of Buena Vista in northern Mexico.
29 March	Scott's forces capture Vera Cruz, Mexico.
18 April	Battle of Cerro Gordo in central Mexico.
13 September	Battle of Chapultepec on the outskirts of Mexico City.
14 September	US forces occupy Mexico City.
22 December	In his first speech in the US House, Whig Congressman Abraham Lincoln calls on President Polk to define precisely where American troops had been attacked on American soil in the actions that precipitated the Mexican War.

1848

2 February	US and Mexican negotiators sign the Treaty of Guadalupe Hidalgo.
10 March	The US Senate ratifies the Treaty of Guadalupe Hidalgo.
12 June	The US Army ends its occupation of Mexico.

1850

| 9–12 September | Five bills passed by the US Congress become known as the Compromise of 1850, primarily dealing with the lands in the Mexican Cession. |

1853

| 30 December | The US and Mexico agree to the Gadsden Purchase Treaty. |

1854

| 4 January | Stephen A. Douglas introduces the Kansas–Nebraska Act in the US Senate. |
| 26 May | Congress approves the Kansas–Nebraska Act. |

PREFACE

BACKGROUND

Between the end of the American War of Independence and the beginning of the American Civil War, the United States expanded in rapid, dramatic fashion. In 1790, the first official census taken by the newly independent nation revealed a population of 3,900,000 living in the lands granted to the United States by the treaty that ended the War of Independence (see Map 1). By 1850, the territory claimed by the United States extended across the continent, from the Gulf of Mexico and the Rio Grande in the south, to the St Lawrence, the Great Lakes, and the 49th parallel in the north (see Map 6). The population in 1850 was over 23,000,000, having grown at a rate about twice that of Great Britain in the same period. Over half these people lived outside the original thirteen states. Despite a population that nearly doubled every quarter century, in a land of bountiful resources this dramatic increase brought not want and destitution, but an economic growth that outpaced the growth of the populace. The westward spread of the American people has been described by one historian as 'one of the greatest folk movements in all history' (Howe, 1973: 94–5).

The purpose of this book is to provide an introductory overview of the story of American expansionism from the end of the American Revolution in 1783 to the eve of the American Civil War in 1860. But besides looking at the basic outline of this historical development, this volume also seeks to answer certain questions about American attitudes towards this territorial growth. Were all Americans in favor of expansionism? How does the concept of a 'manifest destiny' of the United States to expand as a unified nation relate to the growth of sectionalism in this same era? If Americans truly saw expansion as something that was evident or manifest, why was there significant opposition to virtually every expansionary move in this era?

At times, American territorial expansion involved extensive lands being annexed in a single action, such as the Louisiana Purchase, the settlement of the Oregon controversy, the annexation of Texas, or the Mexican Cession. But there were also other examples of American expansionism in smaller increments, such as the numerous treaties for the 'extinguishment of title' from the Indians who occupied lands that the young nation claimed, and the excursions into Spanish Florida that finally resulted in the annexation of that territory as well.

Expansionism was not a new sentiment in nineteenth-century America. Indeed, America was expansionist from the beginning. Diplomatic historian Bradford Perkins has asserted, 'The idea of expansion was born when America was born' (Perkins, 1993: 176). Colonial charters issued in the sixteenth and seventeenth centuries sometimes included grants of land across the entire North American continent, even though no one really knew what lay in the far western reaches of that territory. Throughout the colonial era, British subjects in the thirteen seaboard colonies dreamed of the possibility of expelling France and Spain from neighboring parts of North America. Coupled with this desire for the land itself was the belief that British social, political, and religious institutions were superior to those of the native Indian tribes, or those of the competing French and Spanish empires. Thus, British Americans often thought they had a duty to spread these superior institutions. As historian Robert Johannsen has written, 'destiny and mission have a pedigree that predates the nation itself' (Johannsen, 1997: 3).

The desire of American colonists to expand beyond the Appalachian Mountains was one of the factors leading to the alienation of the colonies from the mother country in the decade or so before the American Revolution. At the end of the French and Indian War in 1763 the British crown had issued the Proclamation of 1763, which forbade settlement beyond the Demarcation Line, which generally followed the western slope of the Appalachian Mountains. The Crown hoped that this decree would prevent conflicts between Indians and settlers in the western regions, but the colonists tended to think they had fought to take this land from France and therefore should be allowed to settle and develop it.

Many Americans would probably cite the Louisiana Purchase of 1803 as the first example of American expansionism. However, there had been dramatic growth in American control over territory in the years between 1783 and 1803. According to the Treaty of Paris of 1783, which ended the American War of Independence, much of eastern North America had been ceded by Great Britain to the United States (see Map 1). However, the Indians inhabiting large parts of this region knew and cared little what a paper signed in Paris said about lands they considered their own. So, to a great extent, the earliest expansionary moves of the United States were the efforts to obtain Indian acquiescence to American occupation of territory that the government believed was officially already its own land.

THE CONCEPT OF MANIFEST DESTINY

In the 1840s, those who supported the expansion of the United States across the North American continent coined the phrase 'Manifest Destiny' as a justification for this territorial aggrandizement. The term meant simply that it was manifest or evident that the United States was destined to expand across the continent. The idea that the United States was destined to develop a large continental empire clearly predated the coining of the term. Both before and after it came into usage in the 1840s many people may have believed in 'Manifest Destiny' without using the term. In the colonial era and in the early republic, there was already evidence of this belief that America would inevitably expand. Ironically, at the same time, there was also an awareness of the fact that republics had tended to be short-lived. Republican government was thought to be a fragile thing that would not survive without a virtuous citizenry. These two beliefs – America's destined greatness and the fragile nature of a republic – while they seem contradictory, nevertheless coexisted in the early national period.

Many different elements are involved in a concept such as Manifest Destiny, especially since the term has been used in a variety of ways and not always consistently. One key element is certainly nationalism. In its simplest sense, nationalism involves a patriotic pride and love of one's own nation. But it also involves giving allegiance to the nation, rather than to a smaller part of the nation or to some foreign or international interest. Nationalist sentiment led Americans to desire the expansion of their nation, and to believe such expansion was right and just.

Another element involved in the development of the concept of Manifest Destiny was the belief that the United States had been specially blessed and was the recipient of a special divine providence. The beauty and bounty of the lands settled by the Americans were no doubt one of the chief reasons behind the growth of this belief. As settlement and political development progressed many Americans came to believe that a special providence oversaw the creation of their unique political institutions.

Connected to this perception of special blessings was the American people's belief that their nation was endowed with a special sense of mission or purpose. Many scholars have argued that this is a secularized version of the Puritans' religious sense of mission. John Winthrop, the first governor of the Massachusetts Bay Colony, said they hoped to build 'a city on a hill; the eyes of all the world will be upon us.' Whether from religious or secular sources, generations of later Americans have expressed a similar belief that the United States has a special mission in the world. Usually this belief involves the idea that American political and cultural institutions, because of their perceived superiority, have to be exported to others around the world so that they may share in the blessings of these American inventions.

Imperial forms of government have generally been thought to lead to a loss of freedom for the people, but Thomas Jefferson and other early American political leaders conceived of American expansion as creating an 'empire of liberty.' According to this theory, the United States would expand, at the expense of neighboring nations or Indian tribes, but ultimately incorporation into America would be a boon for the people of these neighboring lands as they came to share in the American political system and its emphasis on freedom.

In some cases, the arguments used to encourage expansion included an element of xenophobia (fear of outsiders). Many Americans believed that one of the benefits of the Louisiana Purchase would be the removal of a European power from the immediate western borders of the United States, thus lessening the likelihood that the United States might be drawn into European conflicts. In the debates over the annexation of Texas, when the US Senate turned down the first application by the Texans to become part of the United States, advocates of the annexation began to suggest that an independent Texas might become allied with British interests. Thus, America's fear of British power became one of the arguments for bringing Texas into the Union.

Finally, the concept of 'Manifest Destiny' as used by American leaders and opinion makers during the expansionary times of the early nineteenth century was sometimes expressed simply as a justification of actions. Historian Thomas R. Hietala has argued that Manifest Destiny provided 'an invaluable legitimizing myth of empire' for Americans, giving them the means to justify the taking of whatever lands they desired (Hietala, 1985: 255). Since it was believed that American growth was destined, the argument ran, the nation could hardly be blamed for taking advantage of whatever opportunities presented themselves. Thus, American greed or acquisitiveness was not to blame; the territorial expansion simply 'had' to happen.

THE DEBATE OVER MANIFEST DESTINY

But was American expansion destined? Did it 'have' to happen? Was the growth of the United States across the North American continent really something that proceeded like an unstoppable juggernaut across the early decades of the nation's existence? Or was it a matter of deliberate political, diplomatic, and military policy and endeavor?

Historians today continue to debate the accuracy and usefulness of the term 'Manifest Destiny.' While it may be futile to discuss whether or not the United States really was destined to expand across the continent, there can be no debate that such a sentiment existed in the minds of many influential people in the period examined in this book. However, even when one looks at the speeches and writings of people at the time, the question remains: were these politicians and journalists simply reflecting public opinion, or were they trying to direct and influence public opinion? Were they accurately describing the national state of mind, or were they trying to *create* or *instill* this belief in America's destined expansion in the minds of the people? These questions will be considered in the following chapters that examine various episodes of American expansion.

While the term 'Manifest Destiny' continues to be used by scholars studying the continental expansion of the United States, it has become more of an historical artifact than an interpretive theme. Historians writing today, sensitive to the fact that many incidents of American expansion might well be seen as imperialistic exploitation of weaker neighbors, generally shy away from embracing the idea of America's growth being destined by fate or some higher power. As recently as the 1950s, however, one could still see prominent historians marveling at the 'inevitability' of America's expansion across the continent. Historians Henry Steele Commager and Robert Morris, the editors of the prestigious *New American Nation* series of monographs on American history, wrote in their introduction to *The Far Western Frontier* by Ray Allen Billington, published in 1956, that 'what is most impressive about the American expansion is the ease, the simplicity, and the seeming inevitability of the whole process' (Billington, 1956: xiii).

Even at the time Commager and Morris wrote, other scholars were abandoning the idea of American expansion being inevitable or virtually destined. In 1955, Norman Graebner published his *Empire on the Pacific*, in which he argued that American expansion was the result of deliberate planning by leaders pursuing what they saw as the national interest. In particular he believed that in the 1840s this national interest was aimed at procuring the use of important ports on the Pacific Coast.

In 1963, Frederick Merk published one of the most influential studies on the concept of Manifest Destiny to appear in the twentieth century. In his *Manifest Destiny and Mission in American History*, Merk argued that the sense of a special national purpose or mission was the key to understanding America's expansionary moves. Pursuing their mission to take their democratic institutions to others, Americans sometimes inadvertently got caught up in conflict with other peoples over territory. However, according to Merk, these imperialistic adventures were departures from the central emphasis on mission. While Merk's book has been widely influential and has been reprinted numerous times, more recent scholars believe that the distinction that Merk seeks to establish between territorial expansion and mission is not borne out by the evidence.

Most historians writing today have continued to reject the idea of inevitability and to argue that American expansion did not just happen, but was pursued and directed by the deliberate actions of American political and diplomatic leaders. Even the titles of some recent studies suggest this shift in interpretation. In his *Manifest Design: Anxious Aggrandizement in Late Jacksonian America*, Thomas R. Hietala has argued that America's expansion was a result of the 'manifest design' of various policies in the administrations of Andrew Jackson and his successors. Expansionism, Hietala contends, grew not out of a boundless American confidence, but out of anxieties and concerns about defense and opportunity, and other issues.

Diplomatic historians have likewise tended to see deliberate action, rather than a 'fated' destiny, as the motivating force behind American expansionism. Alexander DeConde, in his in-depth study of the Louisiana Purchase entitled *This Affair of Louisiana*, argues that the acquisition of Louisiana was 'the result of a conscious expansionism or of an imperial creed promoting action' (DeConde, 1976: ix–x). Similarly, David Pletcher, in his *The Diplomacy of Annexation: Texas, Oregon, and the Mexican War*, focuses his attention on the diplomatic actions of President James K. Polk and his administration. Rather than accepting a sense of the inevitability of what did happen, Pletcher looks at several important turning points where American policy makers could have made different decisions that might well have served American interests better.

It is clear that to whatever extent there was a public consciousness of America's destiny to expand, there was also a significant body of opposition. Each of the major territorial gains made by the United States met with internal opposition from some quarter, although the extent of such opposition varied from one example to the next. The growth of sectionalism throughout the nation and the strong states' rights sentiment in the South in the early nineteenth century also calls into question the extent of the American public's belief in Manifest Destiny. While there were always many ready to cheer any addition to the US national domain, the growing divisiveness of the sectional conflict also meant that there were those who thought a division, rather than an expansion, of the American nation might be a very good thing.

CONCLUSION

Each of the following chapters deals with a major event or era in which expansionism played a significant role in the development of the young American nation. America's earliest expansionary moves, involving the lands of the Indian tribes in the eastern half of the continent, were hardly seen as expansion by most Americans at that time – they believed they were just taking possession of land already granted them by the Treaty of Paris of 1783. Beginning with Jefferson's purchase of the Louisiana Territory in 1803, America entered into a phase in which its expansionary aspirations brought it into diplomatic conflict with the major powers of Europe. This continued in the settlement of the Floridas issue and the negotiation of the Transcontinental Treaty, which settled questions concerning the boundaries between US and Spanish territories, and later in the settlement of the dispute over the Oregon country between the United States and Great Britain. Finally, in the annexation of Texas and the Mexican War that resulted, in large part, from that action, the US entered into armed conflict with a neighboring nation over the issue of land and boundaries. While the annexation of Texas and the American victory over Mexico brought vast new territories into the nation, the question of the expansion of slavery into those territories re-ignited sectional tensions that eventually culminated in the coming of the Civil War. After examining these expansionary episodes, in the conclusion we will return to an assessment of the issue of American expansionism, and will suggest answers to the questions that have been posed here. Finally, a section of documents from the time period studied and a guide to further reading will aid the reader who wishes to further examine the story of American expansionism.

CHAPTER ONE

EARLY AMERICAN EXPANSIONISM

The earliest examples of the expansionism of the young American nation were the conflicts, negotiations and treaties with the various Indian nations in eastern North America concerning the lands between the Appalachian Mountains and the Mississippi River. This chapter briefly surveys the earliest expansionary policies of the United States government in the period between the end of the American Revolution and the beginning of Thomas Jefferson's administration in 1801.

In the Treaty of Paris of 1783, which ended the American Revolution, Great Britain had agreed to generous boundaries for the newly independent United States (see Map 1). The American commissioners sent to negotiate the peace had been instructed by the Continental Congress to insist only on independence. In other matters, they were to follow the lead of America's French ally. But the American negotiators soon found that French interests and American interests did not necessarily coincide. France hoped that an independent United States would weaken the British Empire, and that the young American nation would remain a weak dependent of France in the international arena. Spain, which had entered the war against Great Britain late as an ally of France (but never directly allied to the United States) wished to restrict America's ability to expand to the West. The Spanish negotiators suggested that the lands between the Appalachian Mountains and the Mississippi River be reserved for the Indians, an idea which also appealed to the British negotiators.

Faced with these difficulties, the American peace commissioners decided to disregard their allies and negotiate with the British directly. This created virtually a separate peace between the United States and Great Britain. While the American negotiators did not get all they wanted, they got more than many observers at the time anticipated. The boundaries agreed to in the Treaty, generally from the St Lawrence River south to the 31st parallel, and from the Atlantic coast west to the Mississippi River, granted the United States a sizeable western domain that had never been a part of the original thirteen states. The United States was taking control of approximately 541 million acres of land, about 230 million acres of that total being west of the Appalachian Mountains. This region between the Appalachian Mountains and the Mississippi River was an area of great potential interest to American settlers.

After the Revolution, not only were settlers interested in these rich lands, but also the new national government was very eager for the settlers to go to this region and to purchase land from the national domain. Under the Articles of Confederation, the US government lacked any efficient powers of taxation, so revenue problems were a recurring concern. Cash from the sale of public land was the major source of federal income; thus the young nation was vitally interested in seeing settlers take up the land. Land was also needed to redeem the bounties that had been given to soldiers during the Revolution as an encouragement to enlist or to remain in the army.

DISPOSSESSING THE EASTERN INDIANS

The nations involved in colonizing North America generally proceeded under the assumption of the 'royal estate' principle. What the Europeans considered 'undiscovered' lands were claimed in the name of the monarchs under whose flag the discoverers sailed. Thus, the land was thought to belong to the nation that had first laid claim to it. The French had first claimed much of the Ohio River Valley, although the British disputed French control over the eastern portions of this region. In 1763, France had ceded its rights to this land as part of the settlement that ended the Seven Years' War and its American counterpart, the French and Indian War. Twenty years later, at the conclusion of the American Revolution, Great Britain ceded much of this land to the United States.

Thus, according to established diplomatic practices in the European tradition, the leaders of the United States believed that they had a legitimate claim to these lands. But the Indian tribes inhabiting the lands generally saw the issue otherwise. Many tribes denied that either the French or the British imperial governments had ever conquered them, and therefore the British had no right to cede these lands to the United States.

However, before the federal government could deal effectively with the Indians' claims to the western lands, it first had to deal with the claims of several of the states within the Union. In the midst of the War of Independence, the Articles of Confederation had been drawn up as a form of government for the new nation. The Continental Congress approved the Articles in November 1777, but formal adoption required the unanimous consent of all of the thirteen states. The state of Maryland held up ratification of the Articles for four years because of a dispute over the western lands issue. Several of the states had extensive claims for lands west of the Appalachian Mountains, dating from their original colonial charters. But some of the states, such as Maryland, had no western land claims. Politicians in Maryland believed that the states without western lands would continually be at a disadvantage in this new union, as compared to the states with large land claims. Therefore, Marylanders insisted that all lands be turned over to the federal government. Maryland refused to ratify the Articles of Confederation until the states with western land claims – New York, Connecticut, Massachusetts, North Carolina and Georgia – agreed to cede their claims to the national government. With Maryland's final approval in 1781, the Articles of Confederation went into effect. Throughout its brief history, many problems plagued the government under the Articles of Confederation. Fearful of creating a national government that was too strong, American statesmen had instead created one that was not really strong enough to function effectively. Once the War of Independence was over, the young American nation found that land issues were among the most pressing concerns facing the government. Besides the needed revenue that land sales provided, there was also the basic philosophy that the best use of the government's domain was to get it into the hands of settlers who would bring the land into production. Before the land could be sold to settlers, however, the government had to deal with the issue of the Indians' claims to the land. Approximately half of the territory that Great Britain turned over to the United States in the treaty concluding the War of Independence consisted of unceded Indian lands. Once the Indians were removed or had otherwise given up claim to their land, and the land had been sold to settlers, the government faced the question of how to govern newly settled territories.

In its earliest formulations of policy toward the Indian tribes within the boundaries of United States territory, the new nation proclaimed several goals: peace on the Indian frontier, dealing justly with the Indians, 'civilizing' the Indian people, and providing for their education. Historians continue to debate whether or not these goals were genuinely pursued or were simply political rhetoric. Genuine or not, it can simply be stated that most of these goals were secondary and were never achieved. The primary goal, which was largely achieved over the course of a few decades, was to obtain the title to all of the Indian lands east of the Mississippi River. Since the Indians in this region did not necessarily recognize any legitimate claim that the United States might have over their land, the new government tried various methods to get the Indians to give up their title to this land. This process was often referred to as 'extinguishment of title.'

Besides asserting a right to the land by the established diplomatic procedures represented in the Treaty of Paris of 1783, United States authorities also expressed a more philosophical justification for the dispossession of the Indians. The argument was that the Indians did not *use* the land. American officials argued that the Indians' economy was based only on hunting and gathering, and thus did not make intensive use of the land. Was it right that valuable and potentially fruitful lands should be left in the hands of those who would not bring them into full production? As historian Patricia Limerick has shown, this line of reasoning made the Indians the guilty party: 'The argument thus shifted the terms of greed and philanthropy: it was not that white people were greedy and mean-spirited; Indians were the greedy ones, keeping so much land to themselves; and white people were philanthropic and farsighted in wanting to liberate the land for its proper uses' (Limerick, 1987: 190). As if that ethnocentric rhetorical leap was not daring enough, American policy makers went even further: it was actually in the Indians' best interest to give up the lands. Settlement and development by non-Indians around tribal lands would mean that the game would gradually diminish and 'following the chase' would no longer be possible. Thus, government officials argued, making the Indians give up some of their lands and become farmers themselves was really for their own good. In making these philosophical justifications for taking the Indians' lands, however, American policy makers generally failed to notice that many of the woodland Indians of eastern North America were already agriculturalists to a great degree.

In a series of treaties negotiated between 1784 and 1786, the United States attempted to implement its basic Indian policy. However, Indian leaders often protested the American government's assumption that it already owned the lands involved in these treaties. While a pretense of negotiation was involved, the United States basically dictated the terms of all of these early treaties to the tribes involved. The tribes were told to sign or else face military action, and most felt too weak to resist militarily. By terms of these treaties, the US extinguished the Indians' claim to most of the lands in the southeastern part of what would eventually become the state of Ohio.

In time, the heavy-handed tactics of the government would lead to increased resistance by the Indians of the Old Northwest. Beginning in 1783, a series of Indian wars broke out in the Ohio River valley. Tribal leaders such as Joseph Brant (Mohawk), Little Turtle (Miami), and Blue Jacket (Shawnee) stirred up resistance among the tribes in the northern part of the Ohio River Valley. Eventually they formed a loose confederacy, which historians sometimes refer to as the Northwest Confederacy, to actively resist American advances. Joseph Brant traveled to England to try to get aid for Indians from the British government. British agents in Canada and in outposts still occupied in the Old Northwest did supply arms for the Indians.

THE NORTHWEST ORDINANCES

Even while these Indian wars raged on the northwestern frontier, a significant milestone in the development of American policy toward incorporating these new western lands was achieved with the passage of the Northwest Ordinances of 1785 and 1787. These two bills have been called the most important legislation ever passed by the Congress under the Articles of Confederation. In the Land Ordinance of 1785 and the Northwest Ordinance of 1787, Congress laid out the processes by which the northern part of the Ohio River Valley would be surveyed in orderly fashion, offered for sale by the government, and eventually be organized for territorial government and statehood. The Land Ordinance laid out the provisions for what became known as the 'Rectangular Survey,' the orderly fashion in which the lands were to be laid out into townships and surveyed into sections of 640 acres (a square mile). Most American lands west of the Appalachian Mountains were surveyed by this system, so this legislation laid down an important precedent.

Another aspect of the Northwest Ordinances that was important for the future expansion of the United States was the provision that any states created in this region would become equal in status to the original thirteen states. Once achieving statehood, the citizens in these new states would be equal in all respects to citizens living in the original states. Thus, no class of colonial dependents was to be created in the new territories. Thirty-one of the fifty states that exist today were organized under the principles laid down in the Northwest Ordinances.

The Northwest Ordinances also evidenced a shift in the government's attitude toward dealing with the Indians of this region. Article Three of the Ordinance showed a shift in the government's attitude towards dealing with these tribes:

> The utmost good faith shall always be observed towards the Indians ... their lands and property shall never be taken from them without their consent, and in their property, rights, and liberty, they shall never be invaded or disturbed, unless in just and lawful wars authorized by Congress, but laws founded in justice and humanity shall from time to time be made, for preventing wrongs done to them, and for preserving peace and friendship with them.   (quoted in Prucha, 1984: 1: 47)

While the rhetoric of the Northwest Ordinances in regard to the Indians appeared to be more positive than earlier US policies, one should not overemphasize this shift. As historian Reginald Horsman has pointed out, 'The Northwest Ordinance made it quite clear that, whatever was said to the Indians and however strong the fear of war, the United States intended to settle the area from the Ohio to the Mississippi River' (Horsman, 1967: 37).

CONSTITUTIONAL DEVELOPMENTS

In the late 1780s, problems with the form of government created under the Articles of Confederation finally became so grievous that steps were taken to amend the Articles. Many Americans believed that the government under the Articles was teetering on the brink of failure. If the national government did fall apart, there was a possibility that other nations might move in to try to take control of parts of the dissevered states. Great Britain still had outposts in the Old Northwest, and Spain was active on the southwestern border. An initial attempt to deal with the problems at a meeting in Annapolis, Maryland, in 1786 accomplished little because few delegates from the various states actually attended. But this Annapolis meeting did issue a call for a convention to meet in Philadelphia, beginning in May 1787. Fifty-five delegates, from all of the states except Rhode Island, met in Philadelphia.

The Articles of Confederation required the unanimous consent of all thirteen states for any amendment. It appeared that several major amendments might be necessary, and that unanimous consent might be virtually impossible to obtain. Thus, the delegates to the Philadelphia convention soon realized that their efforts should focus on writing a new framework of government to be submitted for the approval of the people, rather than attempting a wholesale revision of the Articles.

It is not necessary in this context to relate the basic framework of the US Constitution, or the ins and outs of the debates at the Constitutional Convention. But what did the new Constitution mean in terms of the potential expansion of the United States? It created a more truly national government, which could act more effectively for the interests of the entire nation on both the domestic and international scene. The Constitution did provide for the possibility of adding new states: Article IV, Section 3 simply said 'New States may be admitted by the Congress into this Union...' and went on to specify that no new state could be created out of parts of existing states without the approval of the people therein. Since nothing was specifically spelled out about the means of acquiring new territory, most of the delegates may have been thinking chiefly of how new states would be formed in the western regions that were already part of the United States. Historian Daniel Boorstin notes that there was little debate at the convention over this section dealing with the admission of new states (Boorstin, 1965: 265). Delegates from some of the large eastern states argued for provisions in the Constitution that would guarantee that the original thirteen Atlantic seaboard states would always dominate the new government. On the other hand, representatives from the smaller states welcomed the idea that new states created in the west would be fully equal, thus reducing the predominance of some of the large and powerful eastern states (Morgan, 1956: 140–1). The exact details of how new states would be created were left for Congress to formulate in regular legislation.

The adoption of the Constitution symbolized a fundamental shift in the thinking of American statesmen about the potential size of a republic. Originally, many American political thinkers had argued that the history of republics in the past indicated that this form of government was best suited for a small nation. James Madison addressed this argument in the famous essay in *The Federalist Papers*, number 10. He argued that in a large republic, there would be many different interest groups and factions, and the interaction of these different groups would prevent any one party from gaining too much power or influence. Thus, the size of a large republic could be made a favorable point rather than a detriment.

The Constitution provided that this new form of government would take effect when the document was ratified by nine states. That milestone had been reached by June 1788. However, two of the most populous and most economically important states – New York and Virginia – had not yet ratified. Many doubted that any new government would succeed without the full involvement of these two important states, so the implementation of the Constitution did not begin until after those two states ratified in the summer of 1788. The first presidential election under the Constitution was held in January 1789. George Washington was virtually unopposed in the election for the first president under the new framework of government. The first Congress of the new constitutional government met in March 1789.

FURTHER CONFLICTS IN THE TRANS-APPALACHIAN WEST

Whether the nation was governed under the Articles of Confederation or the Constitution, the general objective of obtaining title to Indian lands in the trans-Appalachian west was still being pressed. The government's basic objective of getting the land remained the same even though the methods were changing. In July 1787, the Secretary of War Henry Knox reported to Congress that the government had neither sufficient money nor an adequate army to carry on an Indian war. Faced with this financial fact of life, the government decided that purchasing land from the Indians would be cheaper than war. Knox argued that the government should negotiate with the Indians and 'convince them of the justice and humanity as well as the power of the US and of their disposition to promote the happiness of the Indians' (Horsman, 1961: 40–1).

In October 1787, Congress acted upon all these proposals and moved toward a more diplomatic Indian policy. Congress ordered that a general treaty be negotiated with all Indians of the Old Northwest. Funds were allocated for treaty annuities and land purchases that might come from this treaty. Thus, US Indian policy was shifting. The government would attempt to buy the lands from the Indians, rather than insisting on the 'right of conquest.' Despite this change in procedure, the overall objective of acquiring all lands west of the Mississippi River was still in place. This is clearly seen in the instructions sent to the Governor of Northwest Territory in October 1787. The Secretary of War instructed Arthur St Clair, the territorial governor, 'You will not neglect any opportunity that may offer of extinguishing Indian rights to the Westward as far as the River Mississippi' (quoted in Horsman, 1961: 41).

The proposed general treaty was slow in coming. In 1788, Governor St Clair negotiated a treaty with portions of the Iroquois, Wyandot, Delaware, Ottawa and Chippewa tribes. The government's new policy was partially incorporated in these treaties. St Clair told the Indians that though the US claimed these lands by right of conquest, it was also willing to pay the Indians in order to secure uncontested title to the land.

Despite the numerous treaties that St Clair and others negotiated, troubles with Indians along the northwestern frontier continued as settlers poured into the region in ever-increasing numbers. Factionalism and fragmentation among the tribes in the region contributed to these outbreaks of fighting. Factions of some tribes refused to be bound by treaties that purported to deal with their entire tribe. Shortly after the Constitution was adopted, President George Washington called on the states of Kentucky, Virginia, and Pennsylvania to send militia forces to deal with this Indian resistance on the northwestern frontier. This led to two disastrous campaigns. During the summer of 1790, General Josiah Harmar gathered an undisciplined, ill-trained force of about 1500 militiamen. He marched them toward the forks of the Maumee River (the site of present-day Ft Wayne, Indiana). En route, they destroyed several Indian villages and were harassed by Miami, Shawnee, and Kickapoo ambushes. On 18 October 1790, a large Indian force under the Miami war chief Little Turtle struck from ambush, killing nearly 200 of Harmar's men. The remainder of his force fled in what became a disgraceful rout. This ignominious defeat became known as 'Harmar's Humiliation.'

No better fate awaited the next major effort. In the fall of 1791, Washington sent another force – this one under General St Clair, who then led a 3000-man force to Ft Recovery, an outpost just below the Wabash River on what is today the Ohio–Indiana border. Most of St Clair's troops were raw recruits from eastern cities. By the time he fought his first major engagement approximately 600 had deserted. On 4 November 1791, near Ft Recovery, Little Turtle again led the Indian confederacy in a surprise attack, achieving an even greater victory than the previous year's battle. Over 630 soldiers were killed and some 300 wounded. In the rout following the battle, some of the troops threw away their weapons as they retreated to Ft Jefferson, nearly 30 miles away. In terms of the total number of troops killed, 'St Clair's Shame', as this battle became known, was the worst defeat the American military ever suffered at the hands of the Indians.

After these disastrous defeats, President Washington finally found an able commander to lead the fighting against the Northwest Confederacy: Revolutionary War hero General Anthony Wayne. Wayne was a stern disciplinarian and had soon put his command into much better shape. Little Turtle was convinced that the Army finally had effective leadership, and advised the Indians of the Northwest Confederacy to make peace. Furthermore, some of the Indians were disillusioned because aid from the British that they had been led to expect had never materialized. Other tribal leaders disagreed with Little Turtle, so they turned to others for leadership. The warriors of the Northwest Confederacy were then badly defeated by Wayne at the Battle of Fallen Timbers on 20 August 1794. In contrast to the two disastrous earlier campaigns, Wayne lost only 33 men in this battle.

Following the Battle of Fallen Timbers in 1795, Wayne negotiated with the Indians an agreement that became known as the Treaty of Greenville. The tribes of the Northwest Confederacy ceded nearly all of what would eventually become the state of Ohio. In return, the US paid the tribes involved $20,000 worth of trade goods and pledged an annuity of $10,000 to be shared by all signing tribes.

The payments and annuities promised in the Treaty of Greenville were a bargain from the government's point of view. From 1790 to 1796, almost five-sixths of the federal government's expenditure had been connected with the Indian fighting in the west. Over $5,000,000 had been expended. Now, with peace secured by the treaty, these great expenditures might be avoided. Peace would also open the way for settlers who would buy land and increase the government's revenue.

After the Treaty of Greenville, there was a brief calm in Indian fighting on the northwest frontier. This lasted, for the most part, through the presidential administration of John Adams. Although the Indian wars in the east were not yet over, the US government was proceeding rapidly toward its ultimate goal of extinguishing the Indians' claims to all lands east of the Mississippi.

In the region south of the Ohio River, the federal government also faced serious resistance from the Indians who wished to hold back the tide of white settlement. Rather than the dozen or so small tribes that occupied the Old Northwest, the major Indian groups south of the Ohio included five large tribes – the Cherokee, Choctaw, Chickasaw, Creek and Seminole. Because these tribes had assimilated some elements of Euro-American culture, white Americans came to refer to them as the 'Five Civilized Tribes.' The Seminole lived in Florida, which was still Spanish territory, so it was the other four tribes that confronted the US government in the south at this time.

The problems in the southwest were generally similar to those discussed above in connection with the Old Northwest. An additional complicating factor, however, was that in the southeast the government was often dealing with Indians in areas where state governments already existed, and at times there were conflicts between state and federal officials over policy and matters of jurisdiction.

Whereas Americans feared British interference with the Indians in the Old Northwest, in the south they feared what the Spanish might do to incite the Indians. Spanish authorities in Florida and Louisiana hoped that the Indian tribes of the south might provide a buffer between their territories and the American settlers.

The first significant treaties with the Indians of the south were a number of agreements negotiated with the Cherokee, Choctaw, and Chickasaw at councils in Hopewell, South Carolina, in late 1785 and early 1786. These treaties generally sought to draw boundary lines between Indian lands and white settlement, and included promises to keep whites from settling on the lands that were reserved for Indian use. White encroachment on Indian lands, however, was generally the chief cause of troubles over the treaties. Throughout the 1780s and 1790s, the federal government sought to make similar treaties involving other lands with these three tribes and also with the Creek tribe. The victory of Anthony Wayne over the Indians of the Old Northwest at Fallen Timbers in 1794 seemed to have the effect of calming tensions on the southwest frontier also, as the southern Indians realized that the troops that had been tied up in the fighting north of the Ohio now might be sent to fight in the south. Likewise, the Treaty of San Lorenzo in 1795 also had a quieting effect on the southwestern frontier, as Spanish officials no longer tried to incite Indian reprisals against American settlers (Prucha, 1984: 1: 45–6, 69–71).

Henry Knox, who was Secretary of War under the Articles of Confederation government, served in the same position in Washington's administration after the Constitution was adopted. Knox believed that negotiations and purchases of Indian lands would be more economical than fighting. He also believed that warfare would 'stain the national character ... beyond all pecuniary calculation' (quoted in Horsman, 1961: 43). Knox suggested that as white settlement neared the boundaries of Indian lands, the game would diminish. The Indians living just over the border, in lands left to them in the last round of negotiations and purchases, would now find their lands less attractive. They could be induced to sell more land and move further to the west. Over a period of many years, this process might be repeated over and over, and Knox believed that in fifty years there would be virtually no Indians living east of the Mississippi River (Horsman, 1961: 41).

Knox was also a strong advocate of the idea that 'civilizing' the Indians would tie them more firmly to the interests of the government. He supported sending missionaries among the Indians to conduct schools, and advocated laws guaranteeing fair treatment for the Indians in trade. In the early national period, the federal government did adopt several 'trade and intercourse acts' that aimed to protect the Indians from overt acts of violence and exploitation. Regulations were adopted that forbade encroachment of white squatters on Indian lands, outlawed the sale of liquor to the Indians, and set standards for fair trading practices. While the passage of these laws and regulations showed some sign of good intent, enforcement was another matter. In the long run, the government's desire to treat the Indians fairly, to promote civilization and education, and to gradually assimilate the Indians into American society all proved secondary to the goal of extinguishing title to the Indian lands.

As this brief survey shows, the policy of the US government toward the Indians was evolving in the early national period. Despite changes in procedure over the decades, the overall goal of obtaining the land remained firm. Subsidiary goals such as peace, friendship, justice, and civilization were also pursued, but these largely failed. It seems inevitable that these goals would fail. The American government was trying to do two contradictory things: acquire Indian lands in a wholesale fashion, while also attempting to treat Indians justly (at least from the government's point of view). One or the other of these aspirations could have been achieved, but not both at the same time. America discovered early on that 'the lot of a colonizer with a conscience is not a happy one' (Horsman, 1961: 53).

DIPLOMATIC CONCERNS

As the United States sought to extend its sovereignty over the Indians within its national boundaries, it also sought to establish itself as a power to be reckoned with in the international arena. Being a nation greatly interested in maritime trade, the United States eagerly sought favorable trade relations with the major powers of Europe. The great majority of American imports came from Great Britain, and these were allowed to move only on British ships. British possessions in the West Indies and Canada were closed to American ships. Complicating these matters further was the fighting between France and Great Britain that broke out as a result of the French Revolution and would continue intermittently until the conclusion of the Napoleonic Wars.

Supreme Court Chief Justice John Jay was sent to Great Britain in 1794 to attempt to negotiate a trade treaty. The United States wanted much, but had little to offer in the way of bargaining concessions. The issues Great Britain wanted addressed were modest: payment of pre-revolutionary debt owed by Americans to British businesses, and compensation for loyalists who had lost property when they left America during or after the Revolution. Both of these matters had supposedly been addressed in the treaty that ended the Revolution. Given the fact that the United States had little to offer to the British, Jay succeeded in getting a reasonable treaty in November 1794, in which the British agreed to withdraw from the posts in the northwest before 1 June 1796. US vessels were allowed to trade in British East Indian ports, and in West Indian ports with some restrictions. Commissions were set up to deal with the issue of pre-revolutionary debts, boundary questions, and compensation for illegal seizures of ships at sea. In addition, the United States was granted most-favored-nation trade status. Several controversial issues were left unresolved: there was no agreement on the issue of British impressment of American seamen, on compensation for slaves that left the United States with the British army at the end of the Revolution, or on the issue of Loyalists' claims to property abandoned in the United States.

Maritime interests in northeastern states, and especially in New England, believed that the Jay Treaty was a sell-out to the British. Jefferson's Democratic-Republican Party, which was generally pro-French in international relations, also attacked the Jay Treaty for its alleged weaknesses. The Senate had ratified the treaty in a secret session, so protests over it did not arise until after the fact. Partisan attacks on the treaty and the Washington administration were widespread and bitter, but generally short-lived. In the western states and territories, the treaty was welcomed because of the stipulation that British forts in the Old Northwest would be abandoned. Most of the critics eventually came to realize that the United States had not been in a position to expect much more than Jay accomplished in the treaty.

Another important diplomatic achievement that had significant impact on settlement in the trans-Appalachian west was the Treaty of San Lorenzo, also known in America as the Pinckney Treaty. Thomas Pinckney, the US ambassador to Great Britain, had gone to Spain in the spring of 1795 to negotiate with the Spanish over issues involving the Mississippi River and the boundary between the United States and Spanish Florida. The resulting Treaty of San Lorenzo was signed in October 1795. The treaty fixed the 31st parallel as the southern boundary of the United States. Pinckney also acquired a concession on the use of the Mississippi for American shipping. Americans had the right to sail the lower reaches of the Mississippi, and to deposit goods in New Orleans, without paying duty, for later shipment to other ports. Spain also agreed to cease encouraging Indians in the southeast from attacking into US territory.

EARLY SETTLEMENT IN THE TRANS-APPALACHIAN WEST

In the Old Northwest, Anthony Wayne's victory over the Indians at the Battle of Fallen Timbers, followed within two years by the British agreement in the Jay Treaty to give up their outposts in the region, set off an acceleration of American immigration and settlement into the region. Similarly, Pinckney's Treaty and the pacification of many of the tribes in the area south of the Ohio River also set off a rapid migration into that region. From the late 1790s until the onset of the War of 1812, a great flood of settlers began moving into the region between the Appalachian Mountains and the Mississippi River. Two new western states were admitted in the 1790s: Kentucky in 1792 and Tennessee in 1796. In the east, cities like New York, Philadelphia, and Baltimore, which had outlets to the western hinterlands, grew dramatically in wealth and power. Cities without this western access developed less rapidly. Ohio became the first state created in the Northwest Territory in 1803. Settlers came into the Old Northwest from New England, the Middle Atlantic States, and Virginia. Pittsburgh, Pennsylvania, boomed as an outfitting center for these pioneers; 13,000 migrants passed through the town in 1794. Many pioneers from Virginia came via the route of the Wilderness Road, which ran from Virginia through the Cumberland Gap into eastern Kentucky. This route, which had first been used in the 1770s, was made passable by wagon traffic by 1796. Ohio had a population of 45,000 by 1800. Settlement in Ohio progressed so rapidly that it was soon spilling over into what became Indiana. The Indiana Territory was created in May 1801, with William Henry Harrison being appointed the first territorial governor.

When this new wave of westward migration began, much of the choicest land in the river valleys and lowland plains had already been settled by earlier pioneers, or bought up by speculators who demanded higher prices. Many of these new settlers were drawn to the rolling foothills of the Appalachian Plateau. These settlers were not only drawn by the potential of the new lands, but were being 'pushed' out of their homelands by several factors. Many parts of the east seemed overcrowded. In long-settled areas, land prices were high. In New England even moderately good farms sold for prices of $14 to $50 per acre. In parts of the Old South, the growth of large-scale plantations was also driving up the price of land and displacing yeoman farmers. Along with high land prices came high taxes. Additionally, in some cases settlers moved west simply to escape a social order that they saw as too settled and conservative.

The transition from frontier to settled society occurred rapidly in much of the trans-Appalachian west. Fertile lands available at good prices and ready markets accessible by water transportation meant that pioneer farmers could quickly make the transition from subsistence farmers to commercial farmers, growing large quantities of crops and raising livestock for the market. Corn was the principal pioneer crop. It could be ground into meal for local consumption, distilled into whiskey for a valuable product that was not too bulky to transport, or it could be fed to livestock, which could be herded to market.

Even before the Louisiana Purchase virtually doubled America's dominion, many national leaders believed that the lands east of the Mississippi would be sufficient for many generations of growth and settlement. No one envisioned how rapidly settlement would continue to push the frontier westward. At the time the Articles of Confederation were adopted, the seven states which had western land claims turned over to the federal government approximately 233 million acres of land. This was a domain comparable in size to the original thirteen colonies. Since it had taken the thirteen colonies over a century and a half to spread over the land east of the Appalachian and Allegheny Mountains, many Americans no doubt believed the federal government had enough land for generations to come.

The federal government's land policy evolved over several decades, changing to meet new circumstances and the demands of purchasers. Initially, lands that had been declared open to settlement were sold in large blocks at public auction. While there were minimum prices and minimum acreages specified, there were never maximum limits placed on how much land any one individual or company could purchase. The price and the large parcels in which land had to be bought meant that many individuals could not afford these lands. Large speculators and land companies bought up huge quantities, and then re-sold them in smaller acreages. Government lands not sold at auction were then open to private entry at the specified minimum price.

There was much fraud involved in some large-scale land dealings, but the private speculators and land companies that purchased large blocks of government land did serve a valuable purpose. While these private interests charged more for land than the federal government did, they were willing to sell smaller parcels and to offer credit, both of which were important to new settlers. Besides selling farm land, speculators were also important in laying out towns and villages, for the speculation in town site property was even more profitable than selling farm acreage.

When William Henry Harrison entered Congress, he was determined to fashion a new federal land policy that would allow settlers to buy land directly from the government, in smaller parcels and on credit. The Land Law of 1800, also called Harrison's Land Law, accomplished these purposes. The standard price of $2 per acre was retained, but the minimum purchase was reduced to 320 acres. Purchasers could pay one-fourth down, and have up to four years to pay the balance. Thus, 320 acres could be purchased with only $160 cash down-payment. With such favorable terms available directly from government land offices, speculators, except for those dealing with town sites, were largely driven out of the market. In 1804, Congress further reduced the minimum purchase to 160 acres. In general, as will be discussed in a subsequent chapter, federal land policies tended to become more liberal throughout the early nineteenth century.

One fundamental principle did not change until the late nineteenth and early twentieth centuries, and this was the concept that the government's role as a landowner should be to divest itself of the land. It was generally accepted that the land was to be sold to private owners, with secure title, and brought into production. Before the awakening of conservation concerns in the late nineteenth century, no one seemed to envision that the government should hold large portions of the national domain in perpetuity.

At the end of the American Revolution, the peace settlement had left the United States as a relatively weak nation, with an ineffective form of government, but also with an internationally recognized claim to a vast national domain in eastern North America. Throughout the early national period, the United States sought to deal with the pressing problems of dealing with the Indians within its borders by encouraging settlement and turning public domain land into productive farms and villages, and organizing politically the new settlements outside the borders of the original thirteen states. Additionally, the nation sought to pursue international agreements that would clearly define its boundaries and stake its claim to free use of the Mississippi River and the Atlantic Ocean. Much of what was accomplished in these years set precedents for developments throughout later American history. No doubt few political leaders or ordinary citizens foresaw the dramatic territorial expansion that would take place in the next four decades, but in many ways the stage had been set for that growth.

CHAPTER TWO

THE LOUISIANA PURCHASE

A common misconception in American history is the idea that the United States was an isolationist nation until the late nineteenth or early twentieth centuries. As this argument goes, President Washington warned the American people against involvement in international affairs in his Farewell Address, and Americans heeded his advice and generally stayed aloof from foreign affairs until the time of the Spanish–American War in 1898 or perhaps until the First World War in 1917.

While this has been a popular interpretative theme, even a brief look at early American history shows that the United States has never been a strictly isolationist nation. Expansionist issues brought the United States into complex relationships and sometimes conflicts with foreign governments from the very beginning. The quest for national independence led to an alliance with France. In the early national period, the Indian tribes with which the government negotiated for cession of lands were, by the government's own definition, considered to be foreign nations. The concerns that Americans had over Spanish and later French control of the Mississippi led to the negotiations with France that culminated in the Louisiana Purchase. During the French revolutionary and Napoleonic wars, Great Britain and France interfered with American shipping which involved the United States in their conflicts and led to the War of 1812. American anxiety about British traders working among the Indians in the area of the Ohio River Valley and the Great Lakes was also a factor leading to that war. So even in these early years of its national existence the United States was hardly isolationist.

AN EMPIRE OF LIBERTY

Historian Merrill D. Peterson has noted that Thomas Jefferson's two presidential terms might be said to have concentrated on two geographic fronts. During his first administration, the concern was over the Mississippi River, and the efforts to secure the free navigation of that river eventually

culminated in the Louisiana Purchase. During Jefferson's second administration, he tried to deal with the issue of the freedom of the seas, to keep
both Britain and France from harassing American ships and commerce.
That effort was a failure, and set the stage for the coming of the War of
1812, which began during the first term of Jefferson's successor, James
Madison (Peterson, 1970: 745).

Thomas Jefferson believed that expanding the territory of the United
States was expanding the 'empire of liberty' (Peterson, 1970: 771). While
the United States had gained generous boundaries at the conclusion of the
War of Independence, several powers still threatened to hem in the sphere
of liberty, as Jefferson saw it. In the north, the British controlled Canada
and access to the St Lawrence River. Because of the wars between Great
Britain and France, both of those nations were interfering with American
shipping on the high seas. In the far west and southwest, the Spanish presence seemed to block any further US expansion. After the retrocession of
Louisiana from Spain to France, the French were once again a force to be
contended with in the heartland of the continent. Finally, the Indian tribes
also stood in the way of expansion. But Jefferson was confident that the
United States would eventually burst all these bounds, and he believed more
land was necessary if the nation was to remain one made up primarily of
independent, property-owning farmers. Historian Richard W. Van Alstyne
succinctly sums up Jefferson's thinking in this matter: 'Nature intended the
two Americas to be the beneficiaries of American republicanism, and the
achievement was to be the fruit of free and voluntary colonization' (Van
Alstyne, 1960: 87–8).

During Jefferson's administration, the government avidly pursued the
policy of extinguishing the title of the Indians to all lands between the Ohio
and Mississippi rivers. Paradoxically, Jefferson had a genuine humanitarian
interest in the welfare of the Indians but, at the same time, a voracious
appetite for their land. He believed the Indians should give up their
nomadic hunting lifestyle and settle down to agriculture. Like most Euro-
American observers, he failed to note that many of the eastern woodland
tribes were predominantly agriculturalists. Jefferson believed that the wild
game that the Indians depended upon for their hunting lifestyle would soon
be gone, as white settlement moved closer. Therefore, it would be in the
best interest of the Indians to cooperate with the government in learning
agriculture and manual labor trades. Jefferson also wanted to increase trade
with the Indians. He believed that as they became more used to manufactured goods obtained by trade with the Americans, the Indians would be
eager to sell their land in order to fund their purchases of these goods.
Jefferson believed the Indians would eventually be merged indistinguishably
into American society. Jefferson's vision may have had noble (if
paternalistic) elements, but it was not a realistic vision. The land hunger of

white settlers was already creating considerable trouble on the Indian frontier.

Through a series of treaties during Jefferson's administration, American land holdings pressed steadily westward. None of these treaties involved truly huge amounts of land, but the government's goal of acquiring all the Indian lands east of the Mississippi continued to advance toward fulfillment.

CONCERNS OVER THE MISSISSIPPI RIVER

As Americans began to settle and develop the lands west of the Appalachian Mountains, the importance of the Mississippi River and its tributaries as a highway of commerce grew immensely. The Ohio River and its southern tributaries such as the Tennessee and the Cumberland created a vast network for efficient river transportation. Even before the development of the steamboat, the volume of commerce on the river increased many times over. Water transportation was by far the most efficient and least expensive means of moving bulk goods such as farm commodities and natural resource products such as lumber, coal, or other minerals. American commerce moved in a counter-clockwise fashion. Manufactured goods produced in eastern factories and mills moved to the west to supply the new markets created by the rapid settlement there. Raw materials and agricultural goods produced in the interior went down the rivers to New Orleans, then through the Gulf of Mexico and around the Florida peninsula, and back up the coast by ship. It was cheaper to move these goods many hundreds of miles by water, rather than a few hundred miles overland. Thus, keeping the Mississippi River open to American shipping was vitally important. Jefferson noted in 1802: 'There is on the globe, one single spot, the possessor of which is our natural and habitual enemy. It is New Orleans, through which the produce of three-eighths of our territory must pass to market' (quoted in Paterson and Merrill, 1995: 100).

But keeping the Mississippi open to American commerce was never a certainty as long as any other nation controlled the mouth of the river at New Orleans. France had controlled the Mississippi Valley until the end of the Seven Years' War, when the settlements ending that conflict ceded this land to Spain. In 1795, Thomas Pinckney had negotiated an important treaty with Spain that defined the 31st parallel as the boundary between Spanish Florida and the United States, and also secured for Americans the 'right of deposit' in New Orleans. Diplomatic historian Alexander DeConde has defined the 'right of deposit' as 'the privilege of leaving goods in New Orleans to await shipment in seagoing vessels' (DeConde, 1976: 71).

American settlers west of the Appalachian Mountains were greatly concerned about the Spanish presence in the Louisiana region and their control of the navigation of the Mississippi. There was considerable unrest in Spanish Louisiana in the 1790s. The United States government was reluctant to undertake any action that might take advantage of this unrest, but western American settlers often felt otherwise. The Old Southwest (the region west of the Appalachian Mountains and south of the Ohio River) was a politically volatile region. Settlers there appeared eager to take the matter of Spanish control of Louisiana into their own hands, or to cooperate with French filibusterers who might attempt to invade and take control of the region.

But Spain's days as master of Louisiana were numbered. In the context of the Napoleonic wars in Europe, Spain became allied with France. As the lesser partner in the alliance, Spain was subordinate to Napoleon's wishes. Napoleon, like many Frenchmen before him, dreamed of re-establishing French power in North America as it had been before 1763. Accordingly, he pressured Spain to cede the Louisiana Territory back to France. This was done in a secret agreement, the Treaty of San Ildefonso, in October 1800.

While the retrocession of Louisiana to French dominion occurred in the fall of 1800, Spanish authorities remained in administrative positions in Louisiana. In October 1802, Spanish authorities revoked the right of deposit for American shippers. Americans generally believed that Napoleon's government ordered this, but Spanish officials changed the policy without the foreknowledge or approval of the French.

Even before the right of deposit was revoked, American leaders feared that French control of New Orleans could lead to war with France. Throughout the late 1790s there were rumors that France might regain Louisiana. Even after the retrocession was formally accomplished, secrecy and poor communications kept American policy makers guessing about the fate of Louisiana. When Robert Livingston went to France as American minister in September 1801, the US government still did not know what had happened with regard to Louisiana. Livingston was told that if Spain had indeed transferred Louisiana to France, he should offer to purchase New Orleans and the Floridas from the French. If the Floridas were still in Spanish hands, he was instructed to attempt to get France to put pressure on Spain to sell the region to the United States (DeConde, 1976: 110).

Americans were deeply interested in the fate of Louisiana. Even though the British fleet was troubling American commerce on the Atlantic as much or more than the French were, some believed the French control of Louisiana would make it necessary for the United States to ally with Great Britain in a war against France. People living in the western states and territories were urging Jefferson to undertake military moves to seize Louisiana before the French could regain control. Jefferson had much sympathy for the French and their commitment to republican ideals, but he came to realize that his hopes for an expanding 'empire of liberty' might be frustrated by French control of Louisiana. A French presence in Louisiana might even make it necessary for the US to ally with Great Britain. He wrote a warning to Livingston, 'The day France takes New Orleans, ... we must marry ourselves to the British fleet and nation' (quoted in Paterson and Merrill, 1995: 100). Even as he pursued negotiations for an amicable agreement on Louisiana, Jefferson also expressed the belief that the French would retain Louisiana only as long as the Americans were pleased to allow this. He believed the United States would eventually come to control the territory through 'the force of things' (DeConde, 1976: 112).

While Napoleon and other French policy makers dreamed of re-establishing a French empire in North America, the British initially were determined to prevent this. In 1801, the British foreign secretary informed American officials that Great Britain would not stand by idly and see the results of the Seven Years' War reversed. To prevent the re-establishment of French power, the British might seize New Orleans themselves, with the intention of selling it to the United States once peace was established in Europe. In response, American officials informed the British that the United States was content to see Louisiana remain in Spanish hands, but would not be willing to see anyone else except the US take possession of it. In private correspondence, Jefferson's secretary of state James Madison was even more blunt. Britain already flanked the United States on the north, he said, and would be 'the last of Neighbors that would be agreeable to the United States' in the Louisiana region (quoted in DeConde, 1976:109–10).

AN INCREDIBLE OFFER

The revocation of American shippers' right of deposit in New Orleans created a crisis in the United States in regard to the Mississippi River valley. Because of the necessity of controlling the mouth of the Mississippi at New Orleans, Jefferson authorized negotiations with France for the purchase of New Orleans. In January 1803, he sent James Monroe to Paris to assist ambassador Robert Livingston in negotiations. The American representatives were authorized to make an offer of $2 million for New Orleans. If the French would not sell just New Orleans, then an offer of $10 million could be tendered for New Orleans and West Florida. In his instructions to Monroe, Jefferson solemnly noted, 'on the event of this mission depends the future destinies of this republic' (quoted in Whitaker, 1962: 207).

Monroe arrived in Paris in April 1803. Livingston, acting on his earlier instructions, had already approached French officials about the possibility of buying New Orleans. Upon Monroe's arrival, Livingston reported that Napoleon's foreign minister, Charles Talleyrand, had already made a surprising offer to sell all of the Louisiana Territory (see Map 2). Although they had no authorization from the American government to make such a commitment, Livingston and Monroe believed this was an offer too good to ignore. They agreed to the purchase, although the precise boundaries of the Louisiana Territory were not defined. Later, American statesmen would try to use the vague status of the boundaries as a pretense for the argument that the purchase had included West Florida. French and American negotiators reached agreement on a draft treaty on 30 April 1803. Both sides were interested in quickly sealing the deal, before British or Spanish interference could cause trouble.

Monroe immediately wrote to James Madison, informing him of the incredible French offer and asking for permission to proceed officially with the negotiations. Madison replied in a letter of 25 June 1803, authorizing the negotiations and noting that no instructions had been given earlier on this matter simply because the possibility of such an offer had not been foreseen.

Spain opposed the potential sale, arguing that since Napoleon had not fulfilled terms of the earlier treaties by which France was to regain Louisiana, the land therefore still belonged to Spain. Napoleon had promised to install a Spanish ruler on the throne of a new kingdom in Italy, Etruria, and had never accomplished this. The French had also agreed not to transfer the region to a third party. Spanish representatives asked France to revoke the treaty of sale to the United States, and even offered to pay the same amount the US had agreed to, in order to get Louisiana back. However, shortly after the sale of the Louisiana Territory to the US was finalized, Britain declared war on France over the presence of French troops in Holland. Spain then realized that further protests over the Louisiana question would no doubt fall on deaf ears, as European governments became more concerned about the renewal of conflicts within Europe (DeConde, 1976).

Eventually, the French agreed to a total price of $15,000,000 for all of the Louisiana Territory. This included a payment of 60 million francs to France, which amounted to $11,250,000 in US dollars. Working through the London banking firm of Baring Brothers, and Hope and Company of Amsterdam, the US agreed to pay in bonds bearing 6 percent annual interest and not redeemable for 15 years. The United States also agreed to assume claims that American citizens had against France up to $3,750,000. In a ceremony in New Orleans on 20 December 1803, French authorities officially turned over control of the Louisiana Territory to the United States.

The $15,000,000 total price for 827,000 square miles of land worked out to about 3.5 cents per acre; an incredible bargain. Why was Napoleon willing to sell at such a bargain price? Several reasons might be advanced. James Monroe believed that the strong reaction of Americans against the revocation of the right of deposit may have given Napoleon the 'first and decided impulse' to consider making the sale. Americans were threatening to regain the use of the Mississippi by force if necessary, and Napoleon knew they could do it. This awareness, followed quickly by Jefferson's offer for the purchase, clinched Napoleon's decision.

Other factors included Napoleon's continuing need for money to carry on the war in Europe, the failure of French imperial policy in putting down the revolts in Santo Domingo, and the possibility of similar slave uprisings occurring in Louisiana. By 1803, casualties among French troops in Santo Domingo would reach 50,000. Napoleon was shrewd enough to see that, with the British fleet commanding the seas, he could not hope to defend Louisiana. Great Britain could possibly strip the territory from France. Alternatively, but perhaps more likely, the Americans might decide to take it by force and the British fleet would prevent Napoleon from getting French troops there to defend it. Napoleon commented, 'I have scarcely recovered it when I must expect to lose it' (quoted in Paterson and Merrill, 1995: 102). Perhaps Napoleon took some comfort from the fact that he believed that the accession of Louisiana would help the United States become stronger *vis-à-vis* Great Britain. One of his advisers recalled that Napoleon commented, 'I have just given to England a maritime rival, that will sooner or later humble her pride' (quoted in Paterson and Merrill, 1995: 103).

RESPONSES TO THE PURCHASE

While Jefferson recognized the French offer as a tremendous bargain that could not be passed up, he was troubled by the legality of the transaction. In the 1790s, as partisan strife developed between what became the Federalist Party and Jefferson's Democratic-Republican Party, Jefferson and his political ally James Madison had argued for a strict constructionist approach to interpreting the US Constitution. When Washington's Secretary of the Treasury, Alexander Hamilton, had proposed a national bank, Jefferson and Madison argued that the Constitution did not specifically authorize the creation of such an institution, so it could not be done. Hamilton and the Federalists argued the loose constructionist view that, since the Constitution did not forbid such an institution, Congress therefore had the implied powers to create it.

Initially, Jefferson sought to hold to his strict constructionist views. He believed that a constitutional amendment would be necessary to make the purchase clearly permissible. His advisers cautioned him against such a course, since an amendment might take years to work its way through the ratification process. Eventually, Jefferson came to a pragmatic conclusion. He would proceed with the purchase. If the people believed he had exceeded his proper powers, they would have their say in the election of

1804. The Democratic-Republican members of Congress were instructed not to raise the constitutional issue during the debates over ratification of the purchase treaty.

Jefferson's Federalist opponents initially raised many criticisms about the purchase. A Boston newspaper that was a Federalist party organ called the Louisiana region 'a great waste unpeopled with any beings except wolves and wandering Indians,' and further complained, 'We are to give money of which we have too little for land of which we already have too much' (quoted in LaFeber, 1993: 9). Alexander Hamilton, a leader of the Federalist opposition, favored US acquisition of the territory, but could not bring himself to give Jefferson any credit for it. The purchase was simply a 'fortuitous providence' which was not due to any wisdom or exertions of the Jefferson administration (quoted in Paterson and Merrill, 1995: 105). Jefferson enjoyed pointing out the inconsistency of some Federalist critics. Before the purchase, he noted, some of his opponents saw the region as so rich and important that we should go to war to take it. After the purchase, in the eyes of these critics, it had suddenly become a worthless desert (DeConde, 1976: 178–9). Federalist opposition waned fairly rapidly, however, and congressional approval of the purchase was never seriously in doubt.

The statistics concerning the Louisiana Purchase are truly remarkable. The purchase increased the size of the United States by approximately 140 percent. Although the boundaries were not precisely defined in some areas, what was generally recognized as the purchase area encompassed approximately 828,000 square miles. While the purchase price of $15,000,000 was a remarkable bargain, the United States went into tremendous debt to make the purchase. To put the $15,000,000 purchase price into perspective, it might be compared to the federal budget of the United States government in that era, which totaled only $5 to $9 million annually. By the time the interest on the debt was paid, the actual cost was approximately $27,000,000.

THE LEWIS AND CLARK EXPEDITION

Even before the Louisiana Purchase treaty was ratified, Jefferson had persuaded Congress to appropriate $2,500 to finance an exploratory expedition across the continent. The major purposes of this expedition were to explore feasible overland trade routes and to gather scientific data about the natural resources of the region. Jefferson was a skilled amateur scientist, and had a long-standing interest in the natural history of the North American continent. Reading his detailed instructions for the leaders of the journey, one gets the impression that he would have liked to go on the journey himself. He planned the details of the trip minutely, and listed the supplies he believed they would need.

The leaders selected for this expedition were Meriwether Lewis and William Clark. Both men were military veterans, having served under General Anthony Wayne in the fighting against the Indians of the Northwest Confederacy in the 1790s. Lewis was a neighbor of Jefferson's on his Virginia plantation, and had also served as private secretary to the president early in Jefferson's administration. William Clark, a younger brother of a famous Revolutionary War hero, George Rogers Clark, was a friend of Lewis's and had commanded the military unit with which Lewis had served.

With a picked crew of about 40 men, Lewis and Clark sailed down the Ohio River in the fall of 1803, and then up the Mississippi to St Louis, Missouri. Across the river from St Louis, they built a winter camp in present-day Illinois. While waiting for favorable weather to begin in the spring, the crew trained for the upcoming expedition.

With a keelboat and a number of canoes or pirogues, the party left St Louis on 14 May 1804 (see Map 2). The Corps of Discovery, as the party was called, included soldiers, hunters, and guides. Clark also took along York, one of his black slaves. York proved to be a source of fascination to many of the Indians of the interior west, who had never seen a black person. Among some of the tribes, the color black was associated with great bravery, so some of the Indians believed that York must have been a heroic warrior.

The expedition rowed, poled and pulled their boats up the Missouri River. It took them all summer and much of the fall to get to the Mandan villages, near present-day Washburn, North Dakota. They spent the winter of 1804–5 among the Mandan, staying near the tribe's villages in a winter encampment they named Fort Mandan. The Mandan were agriculturalists who excelled in growing corn in the Missouri River valley. Their villages had long been a center of trade between Indians and Euro-American fur traders, and between various tribes as well. Traders had previously come up the Missouri as far as the Mandan villages, and French and British traders came there from Canada as well, so much was already known about the lower reaches of the Missouri. Thus, the most important part of Lewis and Clark's expedition was the journey from Ft Mandan on to the Pacific Coast.

While at the Mandan villages, Lewis and Clark hired a number of fur traders to go on west with them as guides and interpreters. One of these men, Toussaint Charbonneau, took along his wife Sacajawea. She had been captured from the Shoshone Indians. Clark noted in his journals that her presence with the expedition assured other Indians of their peaceful intentions, since women never accompanied Indian war parties.

In the spring of 1804, the expedition sent the keelboat and several of the men back to St Louis, with reports and specimens to be taken to

President Jefferson. The remainder of the party pushed on up the Missouri. Coming among the Shoshone in present-day Montana, they traded for horses with relatives of Sacajawea. Going overland through the Rocky Mountains, they crossed the continental watershed, and found streams that ran toward the Pacific Coast. The route through the Rockies to rivers that ran west toward the coast was much longer and more difficult than the explorers had hoped. Rather than an easy portage of a few miles, they found a route 340 miles long; 140 miles were over mountains so high that they never lost their snowcaps. Eventually, they reached the Snake River. After building boats, the expedition again became water-borne, and floated down the Snake and into the Columbia River. In November 1805, they reached the mouth of the Columbia on the Pacific coast in what is now the state of Oregon.

They spent four and a half months exploring the coastal region. On a large pine tree near the coast, Clark carved his name and the words 'By land from the U. States, 1804 & 1805.' Returning from the coast, they basically retraced the same route until they reached the Bitterroot River in western Montana. There Lewis and Clark separated, each taking a portion of the party with them, to see if they could find a better route across the Continental Divide. Clark explored the region around the Yellowstone River; Lewis took a more northerly route and went up the Sun River. The two parties reunited on the Missouri River below the mouth of the Yellowstone. Lewis had been shot in the buttocks by one of his own men in a hunting accident; Clark's party had lost all of their horses, apparently stolen by Indians.

Near the mouth of the Yellowstone, the party met two trappers from Illinois, who had come up the Missouri and spent the winter with the Sioux. The trappers went back to Ft Mandan with the expedition. When the Corp of Discovery prepared to leave for the trip back to St Louis, one of the men, John Coulter, asked to be released from his service with the expedition. He went back into the mountains with the party of trappers they had met, and became one of the first of the legendary 'Mountain Men.'

Lewis and Clark arrived back in St Louis in September 1806. The journey was a round trip of some 8,000 miles from St Louis to the Pacific Coast and back, and had taken 28 months (Ambrose, 1996: 404). Incredibly, only one man had died on the entire journey. He died of a burst appendix, which, given the state of medical practice in that day, would probably have killed him even if it had happened in one of the major cities of the United States.

The party received aid along the way from many Indian tribes – the Mandan, Hidatsa, Shoshone and Nez Perce. There was never any violence between the explorers and the Indians along the way, although there was one uneasy encounter with some Dakota (Sioux) Indians in present-day

South Dakota early in the journey. Many of the tribes that Lewis and Clark encountered in the inter-mountain region were virtually untouched by contact with Europeans or Americans. On the Northwest Coast, the situation was different; there the Indians had long been acquainted with sea-borne traders.

EARLY SETTLEMENT AND DEVELOPMENT

While the fur trade and the Lewis and Clark expedition created much interest in the northern and western parts of Louisiana, early settlement in the region was limited to the more central and southern parts of the territory. Sizeable settlements already existed at St Louis and other places along the Mississippi, and New Orleans had been a major port for decades. When the United States took control of the region, it was estimated that the population was between 60,000 and 100,000. The majority of these were Indians and blacks. The largest segment of both the white and black populations were around New Orleans; most of these blacks were slaves but there were a small number of free blacks. In the settlements along the Mississippi, settlers came from a variety of backgrounds – French, Spanish, German, and American.

The purchase treaty between France and the United States provided that the residents of Louisiana were to become American citizens. However, this did not immediately happen even for the Euro-American people in the region. Congress passed a bill in March 1804, for the territorial organization of the purchase area. Along the line that later became the border between the states of Louisiana and Arkansas, the region was divided in two. Below this line was the Territory of Orleans. Since the area around New Orleans was already an important commercial center, this region achieved statehood relatively quickly, becoming the state of Louisiana in 1812. North of this line was the District of Louisiana. Over the following decades, much of this region would be divided up into various territorial entities; some areas would not become states until many years later. After Louisiana was admitted, no new state from the Louisiana Purchase region would apply for statehood until Missouri did in 1819.

Missouri's application for statehood led to the re-emergence of the slavery issue on the national scene. For the next two and a half years, the debate over Missouri dominated all other Congressional actions. The issue was much larger than simply whether Missouri should be slave or free. The dispute could also endanger other compromises over the slavery issue that had been worked out over the years since the Revolution. From the time of the Revolution until 1819, nine new states had joined the Union. Congress had generally brought states into the Union with an eye toward carefully maintaining sectional balance between slave and free states. This balance was very important to the south, because it kept the south on a par with the north in the number of seats the region held in the Senate, since all states were represented equally in the Senate. The greater population and more rapid growth of the north was already causing the north to pull away from the south in terms of the numbers of seats the region controlled in the House of Representatives. Before Missouri applied for statehood, the sectional balance was equal, with each region having eleven states. The citizens of Missouri applied for admission to the Union as a slave state, and thus accepting Missouri statehood would tip the scales in favor of the slave states. But more than just the balance issue was involved. The location of Missouri was also an issue. It was roughly on the same latitude of free states such as Ohio, Indiana and Illinois. The Ohio River was the boundary between slave and free states in much of the Midwest; if the general line of the Ohio's flow was projected across the map to the southwest, Missouri clearly appeared to be an area that should be free. Admitting Missouri as a slave state, then, would thrust slavery further into northern territory.

The debate over admission of Missouri was also intense because the nature of the debate was changing. In earlier times, many people in both the north and the south had agreed that slavery was a necessary evil. But the growth of antislavery sentiment in the north was changing these views. More and more northern people came to see slavery as simply an evil about which no compromise was possible. Attitudes were also changing in the south; slavery was no longer viewed as a necessary evil, but was defended as something positive, as southern apologists developed the defense of slavery on paternalistic grounds.

A compromise on the admittance of Missouri was finally achieved in 1820 under the leadership of Speaker of the House Henry Clay. A solution to the question of the balance of free and slave states was found in the creation of Maine as a new state. Maine was originally part of Massachusetts (although not physically connected to Massachusetts after the creation of New Hampshire), but the people of Maine believed that the state legislature in Boston tended to ignore their interests and concerns, so there was considerable sentiment for separating from Massachusetts and creating a new state. The US Constitution allows this kind of division of a state as long as the people of both the original state and the new state both favor the action. Maine was created as a free state, so, when Missouri was admitted as a slave state, the sectional balance was maintained with twelve free states and twelve slave states (see Map 3).

As to the question of the northern extension of slavery, Congress agreed that Missouri would be allowed to be a slave state, but in the remainder of the Louisiana Purchase, slavery would not be allowed north of the line of 36° 30′ – the latitude of the southern boundary of Missouri (exclusive of the Missouri boot heel in the southeast corner of the state).

Many Americans rejoiced at the settlement of the sectional concerns involved in the Missouri Compromise, but even a cursory glance at a map of the territory involved should suffice to demonstrate that the troubles were not settled, but only delayed. North of 36° 30′, there was a huge territory left open for potential free states. However, south of that line, there was very limited room for the expansion of slave states. In fact, only one more slave state would be created out of the Louisiana Purchase territory – Arkansas, which was admitted in 1836. In the 1830s, what is today Oklahoma was set aside as an Indian Territory, where Indians from the southeast were resettled as part of the Indian Removal program. Because some of those southern Indian tribes did own black slaves, slavery existed in the Indian Territory, but Oklahoma did not become a state until the early twentieth century. The potential free territory, as compared to potential slave state territory, was so out of balance that one must question why southern politicians accepted the compromise at all.

Although there was general rejoicing in America when the Missouri Compromise was reached, there were also many who looked upon the matter with foreboding. Thomas Jefferson wrote, 'This momentous question, like a fire bell in the night, awakened and filled me with terror. I considered it at once as the knell of the Union.' John Quincy Adams, the secretary of state at the time, wrote in his diary, 'I take it for granted that the present question is a mere preamble – a title page to a great, tragic volume' (quoted in Leckie, 1993: 396–7).

SIGNIFICANCE OF THE LOUISIANA PURCHASE

Americans have traditionally looked upon the Louisiana Purchase as a fortuitous happenstance. 'Out of European distress came American success' was the interpretive formula often advanced to explain the circumstances of the purchase. Even a recent textbook (copyright date 2000) heads the section dealing with the purchase with the title 'The Windfall of Louisiana.' Certainly Jefferson's Federalist opponents, even when they approved of the purchase, never gave him credit for any great wisdom or skill in bringing about the acquisition. However, a more realistic appraisal reveals that America actively pursued the acquisition of Louisiana. While it is true that the instructions given to Monroe and Livingston did not envision the possibility of the entire region being offered for sale, it is also clear that most American statesmen seemed to sense that the region would certainly not remain forever outside of American control. When Jefferson sent Monroe to France to discuss buying New Orleans, and perhaps West Florida, he also sent troops to the border of the Louisiana region, in case it became necessary to use military force to seize the territory.

While it would be decades before states began 'advancing compactly' across the lands of the Louisiana Purchase as Jefferson envisioned, the acquisition of Louisiana set the stage for the further growth of a maturing republic. The vast open lands west of the Mississippi also suggested a solution to a problem that vexed every president in early America: what to do with the Indians that delayed settlement and development in the east? From Jefferson on, presidents began to consider and then to implement the idea of moving tribes from the east out to the far western borders of the United States – where it was believed they would certainly be out of the way of the advancing tide of white settlement.

The Louisiana Purchase not only greatly enlarged the United States, but also changed the way that Americans and outsiders perceived the nation. After the purchase, with the nation more than doubled in size and in firm control of the vital Mississippi River, the United States seemed on a more secure footing. References to the concept of the fragile nature of a republic declined; journalists and politicians spoke more of a glorious destiny in store for the nation. A few years later the War of 1812 began, which some historians have called a second war of American independence, and the outcome of that war seemed to be a reassertion of American sovereignty. After that conflict, the United States entered an era of intense, growing nationalism, which seemed vindicated in the minds of many by the remarkable territorial growth of the Louisiana Purchase, the continued dramatic population growth and robust economic development, and the achievement of at least a stand-off with Britain in the war. The United States was emerging as a force to be reckoned with on the world scene.

CHAPTER THREE

ROUNDING OUT THE NATIONAL DOMAIN: DIPLOMACY AND BOUNDARY ISSUES

In the years immediately following the Louisiana Purchase the United States rounded out its eastern borders, rather than immediately pushing into the new territory west of the Mississippi. Settlement and development continued to transform the area between the Appalachian Mountains and the Mississippi. Indian fighting on the frontier and the War of 1812 slowed this tide of settlement for a time, but after the war, a new burst of American nationalism was exhibited in dramatic economic growth, in the further maturation of American political institutions, in new territorial acquisitions and settlements, and in the self-confident assertion of American national interests in the international diplomatic arena.

EARLY SETTLEMENT IN THE LOUISIANA TERRITORY

During the first decade of the nineteenth century Americans showed little interest in rapidly developing the territory recently acquired from France. Except for the first tier of states west of the Mississippi – Iowa, Missouri, Arkansas, and Louisiana – much of the Louisiana Purchase would remain unsettled until well after the Civil War. The main thrust of new settlement in this era was into the Old Northwest – into the new state of Ohio and what would soon become the states of Indiana and Illinois – and into the Old Southwest region of Tennessee, Alabama and Mississippi.

Although settlers showed little immediate interest in the Louisiana Purchase, Americans were interested in learning about the resources of the region. The Lewis and Clark expedition, discussed in the previous chapter, was only the first of several government efforts to learn more about the land it had purchased. Zebulon Pike, an American army officer, was important in the exploration of the northeastern and southwestern portions of the Louisiana Purchase. In 1805, Pike explored the region around the headwaters of the Mississippi in what is today Minnesota (see Map 2). He purchased a small piece of land from the Sioux for a military encampment; this became Ft Snelling, around which the settlement of St Paul eventually developed.

In the summer of 1806, Pike set out on an exploration of the southern plains region, in an attempt to survey the southwestern boundary of the Louisiana Purchase. He explored the Red River of the South, and the northern reaches of the Rio Grande (see Map 2). Spanish authorities suspected him of spying, and he was arrested in February 1807. Since no charges of espionage were proven, he was released, escorted out of Spanish territory, and taken to the American settlement at Natchitoches in Louisiana. The Spanish had confiscated his notes, but from memory he reconstructed much of what he had lost. His reports provided the United States government with some of its earliest information about the south-central plains region. The United States government also sent several other exploring expeditions into various regions of the west in the early decades of the nineteenth century.

The trader often precedes the farmer and the settler in the opening of new lands, and the trans-Mississippi west was no exception to this rule. As noted in the previous chapter, when Lewis and Clark were returning down the Missouri River, they met a party of fur traders who were heading into the mountainous west. The War of 1812 disrupted the fur trade, and immediately after the war there was a depression in fur prices that kept the trade from rebounding for nearly a decade. But by the early 1820s, trappers and traders were once again fanning out throughout the west.

Despite the fact that dozens of fur trading outposts were established throughout the west, the fur trade had only a transitory impact on the settlement of the west. The trading posts were often abandoned within a few years, and moved to other locations, as the fur resources dwindled in a given region, or when Indian resistance proved insurmountable. But the trappers and traders developed a thorough first-hand knowledge of the west, which laid a foundation for later settlement and development of the region.

THE RISE OF THE WEST IN POLITICS

As settlers took up land in the territories west of the Appalachian Mountains, these regions became more powerful and significant in American politics. Western voters quickly made their wants and concerns known. Generally, they favored internal improvements at federal expense, a liberal land policy that favored small-scale farmers and settlers, and the removal of the Indians in their environs to lands west of the Mississippi. The growing political significance of these new western states can be seen in the rise to national prominence of such western politicians as Henry Clay from Kentucky, Andrew Jackson from Tennessee, William Henry Harrison from Indiana, and, a bit later, Stephen Douglas and Abraham Lincoln from Illinois.

In response to demands of settlers, federal land policy became more liberal, from the viewpoint of the purchasers. Over time the government reduced the minimum purchase required, set a standard minimum price, and for a time allowed credit purchases. The Land Act of 1801 reduced the minimum acreage for purchase from 640 acres to 320. Credit purchases were also allowed, but discounts were offered for cash purchases. With these more liberal terms, land sales boomed. Within eighteen months of the passage of the new regulations, settlers, speculators, and private land companies purchased four times more federal land than had been sold in all of the 1790s. The government ended credit purchases in 1820, because of the belief that the Panic of 1819 had been caused in part by speculators buying up government land on credit. In order to ease the problems brought on by the end of the credit system for purchases, the standard price for government land was reduced from $2.00 an acre to $1.25. This would remain the standard price for most of the nineteenth century. In the first four decades of the nineteenth century, nearly 90 million acres of public land passed into private hands.

Some pioneers moved ahead of the official surveyors and land office personnel, settling on government land before it was officially available for purchase. Such settlers were called 'squatters' and in some cases 'sooners' (because they were on the land sooner than they should have been). As early as the immediate post-Revolutionary years, thousands of squatters were already settling on lands west of the Appalachian Mountains. In 1841, to simplify land sales and facilitate settlement, Congress passed the Pre-Emption Act. Under the terms of this bill, squatters, even though they had settled on their lands illegally, were to have the first right to purchase their lands when it did go on sale.

INDIAN CONFLICTS ON THE EASTERN FRONTIER

In the years between the turn of the nineteenth century and the outbreak of the War of 1812, conditions in the region between the Appalachian Mountains and the Mississippi River were anything but stable. A complex mixture of settler demands, Indian resistance, international diplomatic disputes, and finally war buffeted the region. William Henry Harrison was made the territorial governor of Indiana Territory in 1800. He immediately began an aggressive campaign to negotiate further land cessions from the Indians in this region. Mixing diplomacy with military threats, Harrison made numerous treaties for purchases of land. Most of these purchases did not involve large tracts, but altogether they amounted to a considerable part of the Old Northwest. When the Illinois Territory was separated from the Indiana Territory in 1809, this greatly diminished the amount of land that Harrison governed. Therefore he was even more determined to get further cessions from the tribes remaining in Indiana Territory. In the Treaty of 1809, the Delaware and Potawatomi tribes agreed to the sale of three million acres of land along the lower Wabash River. In return, they received an increase in their annuity payments from the federal government and a token cash payment of $1750.

Eventually, Harrison's heavy-handed tactics prompted resentment among the Indians of the region. Tecumseh, a Shawnee leader, and his brother, Tenskwatawa (also known as 'the Shawnee Prophet' or sometimes simply 'the Prophet'), were organizing resistance to American settlement in the Old Northwest as early as 1805. By 1809, the area was on the verge of war. American settlers were rapidly migrating into the lands in the Ohio River Valley opened up by Harrison's treaties. The Indians in the region were scattered, confused, and in many cases intimidated by the overwhelming tide of settlers. In response to this, Tecumseh and the Prophet organized a revitalization movement, calling on the Indians to return to their old lifestyles, to eschew the trade goods of the white man, and to join together in resisting further land cessions.

In 1808, Tecumseh and the Prophet moved to the ruins of Kithtippicanoe, an old Indian settlement on Tippecanoe Creek in Indiana Territory. There they founded a new village that they named Prophetstown. By 1811, about 1,000 warriors were living in Prophetstown. Tecumseh and a delegation of chiefs and warriors went to Harrison's headquarters at Vincennes, Indiana Territory, in 1810. They told Harrison that they intended to keep federal surveyors off of the lands that had recently been ceded in a series of treaties. Tecumseh was successful in blocking any new treaties for about two years.

In November 1811, Harrison led an attack on Prophetstown. After spirited fighting, about 150 Indians were killed. The remainder of the Indians fled, and Harrison's troops destroyed the village. Tecumseh was not at Prophetstown at the time of this attack, having gone into the area south of the Ohio River to try to bring more Indians from that region into his confederacy.

Harrison claimed that British agents in the region encouraged and backed the Indians in their resistance against the American government and settlers. This was a reasonable supposition. Despite the provisions of the Jay Treaty that all British outposts in the Old Northwest were to be evacuated, British traders continued to operate in American territory. These traders supplied the Indians with guns and powder, and encouraged Indians in the belief that Great Britain favored the creation of an Indian 'buffer state' in the Old Northwest – a prospect that seemed to fit well with the message Tecumseh and the Prophet were spreading.

THE WAR OF 1812

The whole issue of what was going on in the Old Northwest eventually became caught up in controversies that led to the War of 1812. It has often been argued that the principal reasons for the War of 1812 were American concerns about their shipping rights as a neutral party as Great Britain and France fought for control of the seas, and British impressment of American sailors into the Royal Navy. In recent years, however, while not dismissing these issues, scholars have paid more attention to some additional factors. These include the desire of settlers in the Old Northwest to end British support of Indians in the region, and the desire of settlers in the Old Southwest to gain access to Florida and the Gulf Coast regions held by the Spanish. Southerners hoped that a war with Great Britain might draw Spain into an alliance with Britain. Spanish involvement then could be cited as justification for American annexation of Florida and the Gulf Coast region that was vitally important to commerce in the Old Southwest. It is interesting to note that when the war finally came, the maritime interests in New England generally disapproved of the war, while the 'war hawks' were usually politicians from the south and the west, such as Kentuckian Henry Clay, John C. Calhoun of South Carolina, and Felix Grundy of Tennessee.

In many ways the fighting in the War of 1812 in the western parts of the United States was basically a continuation of the Indian wars that had been going on there since American independence. The British and the Americans both tried to enlist Indian tribes as their allies for fighting on the frontier. Generally, the British were more successful, because the American settlers seemed to be the most visible problem facing the Indians. One of the most important battles involving Indian allies in the War of 1812 was the Battle of the Thames, in Ontario, north of Lake Erie, in October 1813. Tecumseh was among the Indians who died fighting against US forces there. That battle marked the virtual end of any effective British–Indian alliance in the war.

In December 1814, the United States and Great Britain reached an agreement to end the war, which was formally accomplished in the Treaty of Ghent in 1815. The treaty provided for a return to the *status quo antebellum* – the situation that existed before the war. Thus, neither side gained nor lost any territory in the settlement, nor were the freedom of the seas issues clearly dealt with in the treaty. But the end of the Napoleonic Wars in Europe meant that the circumstances that had led to the maritime troubles were now removed. At the end of the war, the Indians were once again treated as traitors by the victorious Americans. British traders finally left US territory for good, and never again sought to aid the Indians in resisting the expanding white settlement in the Old Northwest. The War of 1812 marked the end of real military engagements between US military forces and the Indians east of the Mississippi except for a few isolated incidents.

DIPLOMATIC DEVELOPMENTS

The era following the War of 1812 was a paradoxical one. On the one hand, it was a time of intense nationalism. American nationalism seemed vindicated by the war with England, even though the war provided no dramatic victories over or concessions from the enemy. At the same time, sectionalism was also a growing force in the United States. There had been tensions between the north and the south from the early colonial days. In the early 1800s, however, a new factor was added – the growth of the trans-Appalachian west as an important section of its own with its own concerns and interests. Both nationalism and sectionalism had connections to American expansionism. Nationalism was obviously a part of the motivation behind 'Manifest Destiny.' But sectionalism was also involved – because every time the nation expanded, there were sectional controversies over the potential expansion of slave or free territory.

The strongly nationalist sentiment in the United States during the years following the War of 1812 can clearly be seen in the diplomatic ventures undertaken by Secretary of State John Quincy Adams. Under President James Monroe (1817–1825), Adams boldly asserted American rights and prerogatives in a number of important diplomatic matters.

The first of the notable diplomatic accomplishments of the Monroe administration dealt with maintaining peace on the Great Lakes. Immediately after the end of the War of 1812, there was considerable anxiety about the possibility of further troubles with Great Britain over the Great Lakes region. For a time, both the United States and the British engaged in a naval armaments race on the Great Lakes. Eventually, both sides came to recognize that such actions might well incite troubles rather than prevent them. John Quincy Adams was the American minister to Great Britain, and would become Monroe's Secretary of State when he returned to the US in September 1817. While in London, Adams began talks with the British Foreign Office over the matter. In 1817 the Rush–Bagot Treaty was concluded, which placed limits on the number of warships that either nation could have on the Great Lakes. The treaty was negotiated by Charles Bagot, the British minister to the US, and Richard Rush, the acting secretary of state in Monroe's cabinet at the time. Although it is often referred to in history texts as a treaty, the agreement was never formally submitted to the US Senate for ratification, so it remained an 'agreement' between the US and Great Britain.

The Convention of 1818, another of the diplomatic successes of the Monroe administration, was an agreement between the United States and

Great Britain dealing with issues concerning the boundary between the United States and British Canada. From the Lake of the Woods region west to the Rocky Mountains, the 49th parallel was set as the boundary. West of the Rockies, in the region known as the Oregon Country, the two nations could not agree on the border, so that region was left open to joint occupancy by citizens of both nations (see Map 3). Besides the native Indians, only a few fur traders from both nations were in Oregon, so joint occupancy was not a problematic issue at the time.

THE ACQUISITION OF FLORIDA

One of John Quincy Adams's greatest achievements as secretary of state was settling matters with Spain over the issues of Florida and the US–Spanish border in the American southwest. The United States remained desirous of annexing Florida, as it was important for navigation because of the numerous rivers that flowed through the region known as West Florida (west of the Apalachicola River) into the Gulf of Mexico. Southerners also saw the area as important for defensive purposes. As long as Spain or any other foreign power controlled Florida, it might be used as a base for attacks into US territory. This had happened during the colonial wars of the seventeenth and eighteenth centuries, and during the American Revolution by tribes allied with Great Britain. Spain had looked upon the Indian tribes in the region as a useful buffer against American expansion into the region. Southern plantation owners were also concerned about Florida being used as a refuge for runaway slaves. As the Spanish empire disintegrated, Jefferson and his Democratic-Republican successors worried about the ultimate disposition of Florida. If Great Britain or France were to come to control it, American access to the Gulf Coast could be threatened.

In his instructions to the American negotiators Robert Livingston and James Monroe in the matter that led to the Louisiana Purchase, Jefferson told the American statesmen to try to acquire New Orleans and West Florida. It was desire for land east of the Mississippi, not west, that was the origin of the purchase. As noted in the previous chapter, there seems to have been a deliberate ambiguity in the descriptions of the eastern boundary of the Louisiana Purchase, which allowed the US to claim that West Florida had been included in the sale. Monroe and Livingston both insisted that they understood the purchase treaty to include West Florida. On the other hand, the French negotiators, knowing that they really did not control Florida, were willing to leave the matter ambiguous.

Jefferson intended to acquire Florida by making a claim that it was included in the Louisiana Purchase and then threatening to seize it. However, he would also make an offer to Spain to forego the use of force if Spain would agree to sell the region. James Monroe was to go to Madrid as soon as the negotiations with France over the Louisiana Purchase were concluded, to attempt to reach a settlement on Florida. Secretary of State James Madison wrote to Monroe, instructing him on what he must tell the Spanish: 'The Spanish government must understand, in fact, that the United States can never consider the amicable relations between them as definitely and permanently secured, without an arrangement on the Floridas' (quoted in DeConde, 1976: 214–15). Despite this strong stance, however, the Spanish refused to even discuss the sale of the Floridas with Monroe.

James Madison, Jefferson's secretary of state, clearly recognized the importance of the coasts of East and West Florida for US commerce. Navigation of the rivers of this region was necessary, Madison said, for 'maximizing' American use of the Gulf of Mexico. The Congressional committee that recommended the appropriations for the Louisiana Purchase also recognized this, and added that to ensure free use of the Apalachicola and other rivers of the region, the US must either purchase or conquer Florida. In February 1804, Congress passed the Mobile Act, the major focus of which was to extend the nation's revenue laws to the Louisiana Purchase territory. However, the bill also asserted US control over parts of West Florida. The legislation claimed US annexation of all navigable rivers within the United States that flowed into the Gulf of Mexico, asserting American control all the way to the mouths of these rivers on the Gulf coast. The bill authorized the president to take possession of the area around Mobile 'whenever he shall deem it expedient' (Owsley and Smith, 1997: 22–3).

Florida was a frequent target of American 'filibustering' expeditions – private forces acting without the explicit authority or approval of the US government. In September 1810, a force of armed Americans led by Philemon Thomas took control of an old Spanish fort in Baton Rouge, West Florida. After meeting with people living in the region, Thomas and his men issued a 'Declaration of Independence' for the region. They sent this document to the territorial governors in Mississippi and the Orleans Territory. Thomas asked that this document be forwarded on to the federal government, and that the US be requested to annex the area and offer protection against Spanish retaliation.

This case illustrated a point frequently involved in such filibustering activities. James Madison, who had become president by this time, faced a difficult choice as to what to do in this matter. He clearly wanted to annex West Florida, but the filibusterers seemed to be forcing his hand at a time that might not be propitious. Madison worried that annexation might arouse enmity with both Spain and Great Britain. However, faced with rumors that Spanish reinforcements were on the way to the region, in late October Madison issued a proclamation that instructed American officials to take control of the region.

During the War of 1812, US forces had made incursions into Spanish Florida and at times occupied parts of this region. Spain was preoccupied with independence movements arising in several of its Latin American colonies and was unable to defend Florida effectively. In 1817, Secretary of State John Quincy Adams began negotiations with the Spanish minister to the United States, Don Luis de Onís, to settle border disputes and define precisely the boundary between the US and Spanish territory. The Spanish crown expected Onís to do whatever he could to halt or at least slow the disintegration of Spanish control in the Western Hemisphere. Onís was to try to keep the US from recognizing the newly independent nations in Latin America, and to discourage any American interest in the Spanish territories on its borders – Florida, Texas and the southwest.

While meetings between Adams and Onís were being held, word was received that Andrew Jackson had invaded parts of both East and West Florida, pursuing resistant bands of Indians on the southwestern frontier. When Onís protested this incursion into Spanish territory, Adams countered that Florida had long been a refuge for hostile Indians, runaway black slaves, and outlaws. Adams suggested that if Spain could not promise order and security on the border, the US might be forced to seize the territory as a matter of self-defense.

United States forces did seize Mobile in 1813. In response, the Spanish governor of West Florida called on the Creek Indians to help repel the American aggression. This caused an outraged reaction among Americans in the border regions. Generally, irregular forces had undertaken the incursions into Spanish dominions – private citizens acting as filibusters. But in this case, regular US forces were involved.

On 14 April 1812, just four days after Louisiana had been admitted to the Union as a state, Congress passed legislation incorporating Mobile and the surrounding region into the Mississippi Territory. The territorial governor of Mississippi, David Holmes, was not informed of this previously, and learned of it only when he read about it in newspapers. He did begin to organize the region, and created a city government for Mobile and appointed a sheriff. Ft Charlotte in Mobile had a Spanish garrison of 130 men; they did not surrender the fort until April 1813. While the force was not large enough to block American moves into the region, the presence of this garrison provided a source of potential conflicts.

Although Andrew Jackson's invasion of Florida nearly derailed the negotiations between Adams and Onís, in the end it served to demonstrate to Spain that the United States could seize Florida if it wished, so Spain finally agreed to sell the region. The final terms of the Adams–Onís Treaty, which was completed in 1819, ceded Florida to the United States in return for US assumption of claims that American citizens had against Spain, up to a maximum of $5 million. In addition, a definitive boundary between the

Louisiana Territory and Spanish possessions in the American Southwest was established. Spain also agreed to abandon any claim to land north of the 42nd parallel. Because it defined the boundary between US and Spanish territories in the west, the Adams–Onís Treaty is often referred to as the Transcontinental Treaty (see Map 3).

THE MONROE DOCTRINE

The diplomatic policy which became known as the Monroe Doctrine was primarily the work of Secretary of State John Quincy Adams, and was his last great diplomatic accomplishment. The United States hoped to remain insulated from European affairs and to deter European nations from interference in the affairs of the Western Hemisphere. As former Spanish colonies in Latin America overthrew Spanish rule and emerged as independent nations, British and American statesmen were concerned that monarchists in some European nations (notably France and/or Austria) might intervene in Latin America to attempt to restore Spanish rule.

In the fall of 1823 British diplomats proposed a joint US–British announcement of a policy to protect the newly independent Latin American states. At the same time, the British warned the French against undertaking any intervention in the Western Hemisphere. French officials assured the British that their nation had no such intentions. To many European diplomats, the threat of European intervention in Latin America seemed to have disappeared with this assurance by the French. Thus, when Monroe announced his Doctrine, many European statesmen saw it as moot; many diplomats also thought the United States was claiming credit for a British policy achievement.

In the United States, President Monroe was inclined to go along with a joint declaration with Great Britain. Former presidents Jefferson and Madison both also supported a joint declaration. However, in cabinet meetings on the issue, Secretary of State Adams argued that such a joint undertaking might appear to be subjecting the United States to British interests, and he counseled rejection of the offer. As Adams put it in his personal diary, the United States should avoid appearing as 'a cock-boat in the wake of the British man-of-war.' His arguments were convincing to Monroe (Adams diary, November 7, 1823, quoted in DeConde, 1978, 1: 126–31).

In December 1823, Monroe announced this policy in his last address to Congress. There were three major points. The first was noncolonization: the United States would not stand by idly if any European nation attempted to form a new colony in the Western Hemisphere. While it was Latin American affairs that prompted the development of the Monroe Doctrine, this particular point was also aimed at Russia, and the possibility of a Russian colony being formed on the western coast of North America. The second point was nonintervention – a warning that European nations should stay out of the internal affairs of any independent Western Hemisphere nation. This was the major thrust of the Monroe Doctrine as it pertained to Latin America. The United States would not abide intervention by European nations in the internal affairs of the newly independent Latin American nations. The third point of the Monroe Doctrine was noninterference. This was a promise by the United States that it would not interfere with affairs between any existing Western Hemisphere colony and its European mother country.

There was really no explicit threat of force in the Monroe Doctrine; the United States did not have the naval might to project any significant power outside its own borders. While Adams had rejected the British proposal to issue a joint statement on protection of Latin America, British backing of the Monroe Doctrine may have been more of a deterrent to other European nations than any threat of American action.

As with many aspects of foreign policy, the Monroe Doctrine can be interpreted in two different ways. The traditional viewpoint has been that the United States was acting on principle and taking a stand to protect the new, weak republics in Latin America by warning Europe to 'keep out' of the Western Hemisphere. However, revisionist historians, looking back on several incidents of American intervention in Latin American affairs, have interpreted the Monroe Doctrine differently. According to this view, in the Monroe Doctrine the United States was announcing that the Western Hemisphere was a US sphere of influence; only the United States possessed the right to interfere with the internal affairs of nations in this region.

BORDER CONTROVERSIES

The question of the boundary between US and British possessions in the Oregon country would eventually become a major controversy in the late 1830s and early 1840s, and is discussed in a later chapter. In the eastern part of North America, the last major boundary issue between the United States and British Canada was settled in 1842 with the ratification of the Webster–Ashburton Treaty. The treaty dealt with disputes over the border between Canada and northern Maine; a region of approximately 12,000 square miles in northern Maine was in dispute. Most of the people living in the region were settlers from the United States, and the area was viewed as a potentially rich logging resource (Merk, 1971: 4, 43–4). The disputes had arisen because the border was not accurately described in the treaty which ended the American War of Independence. The border had been described in detail in that treaty, but the details referred to were not accurately described. Certain geographic features that were supposed to define the boundaries either could not be found or did not fit the surveys made later.

The Treaty of Ghent of 1815, which ended the War of 1812, attempted to deal with the boundary issue by creating a number of commissions to deal with individual issues. These commissions also fail to reach an acceptable settlement due to the confusing descriptions of the geography of the region. Foreseeing this possibility, the negotiators at Ghent had also included a stipulation that should these commissions fail to reach an acceptable agreement, both sides would agree to submit the matter to arbitration by a friendly sovereign or nation, and accept whatever decision was rendered as 'final and conclusive.' In 1827, the King of the Netherlands was asked to arbitrate the issue. He decided that a judicious decision could not be made on the basis of the available evidence, and drew a compromise line that basically split the disputed territory into roughly equal parts. Statesmen from both the United States and Great Britain believed the king had overstepped his authority in the matter and refused to accept the settlement, although the British had been ready to accept the compromise if the US had.

Daniel Webster, a prominent New England Whig politician, had become secretary of state under President William Henry Harrison in 1841. Harrison, the first Whig elected president, died of pneumonia within weeks of taking office. His vice-president, John Tyler, then became president. Webster continued to serve in Tyler's cabinet for a time. By the early 1840s, some southern Democrats were already threatening war with Great Britain over the Oregon controversy and other issues. The Whigs, however, represented the business and maritime interests that viewed Great Britain more favorably. Therefore, Webster let the British know that the United States was ready to attempt to reach a final agreement on the Maine border issue.

In the spring of 1842, British Prime Minister Sir Robert Peel sent Alexander Baring, the first Lord Ashburton, to the United States as a special minister to negotiate a settlement on the Maine border issue. In June of that year, Webster and Lord Ashburton began discussions on the matter. The negotiations began positively in an atmosphere of friendship and candor. However, when the two statesmen actually got down to the issues, they got into involved disputes over geographical features and mapping problems, just as all previous negotiators handling the issue had done.

The major sticking points in the negotiations were the desire of the US to keep all the disputed area, and that of Great Britain in constructing a military road to link Halifax with Quebec. Maine settlers were especially interested in the Aroostock Valley region, which was rich not only in timber resources but in good quality soil for farming. After several rounds of negotiation, which included not only Webster and Ashburton but commissioners appointed by the states of Massachusetts and Maine, and at times President Tyler himself, the boundary agreed upon left most of the Aroostock region in US hands, and the route of the proposed military road in British hands. Of the roughly 12,000 square miles in the disputed region, the United States received about 7,000. Politicians from Maine and Massachusetts protested that too much land was being given up, but the federal government gave each state $150,000 in compensation for the 'lost' lands.

The Webster–Ashburton treaty met with opposition in both the US and Great Britain by those who believed their own country had given up too much. This led to what became known as the 'Battle of the Maps,' in which statesmen in both nations used different and conflicting maps to show that they had not made unwise concessions. The treaty was signed by the negotiators in August 1842, and formally announced by both nations in November of that year.

INDIAN REMOVAL

While the United States rounded out its borders by agreements with Spain and Great Britain, and warned European nations to stay out of Western Hemisphere affairs, it also continued to pressure the Indians within its borders to give up title to the lands they occupied. During Andrew Jackson's administration, a formal policy of relocating Indians from the eastern part of the United States into lands west of the Mississippi was begun. Jackson is the president most often associated with this policy, but the policy had been envisioned long before Jackson took office. As far back as Washington, American presidents had considered the possibility of moving Indians from the east into lands farther west that might not be considered desirable by white settlers.

Andrew Jackson had been involved in Indian affairs for years before he became president, both as a military officer and as a territorial governor. He had negotiated some treaties with the Cherokee and Choctaw tribes on the southwestern frontier. Jackson believed that the Indians had only a simple right of tenancy to their lands. He believed that the policy of negotiating treaties with the Indians as though they were separate sovereign nations was an anachronism, which had been adopted at a time when the government was too weak to do otherwise. Now that the United States was clearly more powerful than the Indian tribes, Jackson believed this policy should be abandoned. Jackson made Indian removal a major campaign issue in the 1828 election, and he was very popular in the west and the south – the areas where considerable numbers of Indians remained.

With Jackson's backing, Congress passed what became known as the Indian Removal Bill in May 1830. The bill gave the president the power to exchange lands in the west for lands held by Indian tribes in the east. The lands in the west were to be guaranteed to the tribes 'forever.' The government would pay for improvements that had been made to the lands being given up in the east, and would provide assistance in moving the Indians to the west. The bill specifically said that no existing treaties would be violated. This meant that new treaties would have to be negotiated in which the Indians agreed to removal. There was no mention in the bill of the use of force if tribes or factions of tribes refused to move.

The Indian Removal Bill engendered both support and opposition from a variety of sources and motives. Support generally followed both party and geographical lines. The northeast, and especially New England, opposed the removal policy. The south and the western frontier states were firmly in favor of it. Those who thirsted for the chance to acquire the Indian lands naturally supported the removal bill. Ironically, however, many philanthropists and humanitarians who believed they were looking out for the best interests of the Indians also supported removal, believing that this would make their lands in the west more secure, with no threat of white encroachment. Additionally, removal would take the Indians away from the 'bad sort' of whites – liquor sellers, dishonest traders, and rapacious land dealers. The Indian Territory in the west would be a kind of haven where the Indians could more slowly adapt and assimilate the manners of white civilization. It seems that no one at the time noted the irony of this proposition – in order to 'civilize' the Indians, it was necessary to move them further away from white 'civilization.'

The land where the proponents intended to move the eastern Indians was a large area of the central plains region in what is now Nebraska, Kansas, and Oklahoma. Since Texas had not yet been annexed, nor the southwestern region acquired from Mexico, this region was the extreme western edge of the United States. Many believed that the Great Plains west of the Missouri River would be largely unsuited to white settlement. The exact boundaries of what was considered the 'Indian Territory' were never precisely defined, but, eventually, an extensive area was reserved for Indian colonization and settlement. Roughly, the boundaries were the Platte River in Nebraska in the north; the Red River in the south; the 100th meridian in the west, up to the Arkansas River, and from there along the Arkansas River to the base of the Rocky Mountains.

Of course, before Indians from the eastern region could be moved to this Indian Territory, the Indians already living there had to agree to give up some of their lands and allow this colonization. The Stokes Commission, chaired by Montfort Stokes of North Carolina, went to the Plains region in 1835 to negotiate with the western tribes. A battalion of cavalry accompanied the treaty commissioners, and was later augmented by the arrival of the Dragoon Expedition. The First Dragoon Regiment – infantry that rode into battle but fought dismounted – was considered the most impressive military force that the United States had ever sent to the Plains region. The American government hoped to awe the Plains tribes by this display of military might.

Between 1835 and 1837, the Stokes Commission held meetings with the Wichitas, Caddoes, Kiowas, Comanches, and other smaller groups in the south-central Plains region. These tribes signed their first treaties with the United States, agreeing to sell parts of their lands to the government and pledging peace with the new tribes that the government would settle on their former domains.

The removal program provoked factionalism among many Indian tribes, as portions of a tribe would agree to move to the west while others refused. By the mid-1830s, all those groups who were going to remove 'voluntarily' had done so. 'Voluntarily' in this context means that while they were not literally forced at the point of a bayonet, they did face heavy government pressure to move.

The removals that prompted the most violent opposition involved the Cherokee and Seminole tribes. The Cherokee lived in western Georgia and portions of North and South Carolina. Many of the Cherokee were highly assimilated, living in frame houses and farming. The tribal government had a written constitution, and a newspaper was published in the Cherokee language. However, the Cherokee faced relentless pressure from white settlers and the state government in Georgia, who wanted the Cherokee to move to the west so that their eastern lands could be opened to white settlement.

Part of the Cherokee tribe's attempt to resist involved appeals to the United States Supreme Court, in which lawyers representing the tribe argued that the laws of the state of Georgia did not apply to them. The first of these cases was *Cherokee Nation v. Georgia*, in 1831. In this case, Chief Justice John Marshall ruled that the Supreme Court did not have jurisdiction in the case. While expressing sympathy for their cause, Marshall argued that the Cherokee were a 'domestic dependent nation,' and as such did not have the standing to bring suit in federal court. Thus, Marshall believed he had no authority to act in the case. In another case the following year, *Worcester v. Georgia*, 1832, Marshall did rule that laws passed by the Georgia legislature did not apply to the Cherokee lands. This decision should have restored some justice to the matter. However, officials in Georgia knew that Andrew Jackson had no intention of requiring their compliance with this judgment, and so they proceeded to despoil the Cherokee lands. In 1834, the Georgia legislature passed a law calling for the Cherokee lands to be surveyed and sold by lottery to any purchasers. The Georgia militia was sent to destroy much of the town of New Echota, which was the capital of the Cherokee nation.

As with many tribes, factions developed among the Cherokee. One group saw removal as the lesser of two evils. This group became known as the Treaty Party. In 1835, this faction agreed to the Treaty of New Echota. Although it was clear that the majority of the tribe did not agree with the treaty, the federal government considered its terms binding on all the Cherokee. In this treaty, the Cherokee ceded 8 million acres for payment of $5 million and a new homeland in the west. Only about 2,000 Cherokee voluntarily emigrated to the west under the terms of this treaty.

Jackson stuck to his guns, however, to see that the treaty was adhered to. 23 May 1838 was set as the removal deadline. Over 15,000 Cherokee remained in the east and had to be forcefully evacuated by troops. The Army rounded up recalcitrant members of the tribe throughout the summer, keeping those already gathered in what amounted to concentration camps throughout the summer while the process continued. Many died from disease in the close confinement of these camps. In the fall and early winter of 1838 the army began moving the Cherokee to the west. Some went in flatboats on various rivers in the south, some on horseback and in wagons, and many traveled on foot.

As the Cherokee traveled the roughly 1,200 miles to the Indian Territory, the autumn rains and chills brought on a variety of illnesses that claimed many lives. It is estimated that about 4,000 members of the tribe – about one-fourth of the total population – died along the way. Besides the physical suffering, the Indians were also harassed by marauding whites along the journey. Traders claimed horses and other possessions as payments for debts; some of these debts were no doubt real but many were fictional. A few hundred Cherokee individuals succeeded in eluding the federal forces and remained in North Carolina, eventually becoming known as the Eastern Cherokee.

The most violent opposition to removal was from the small Seminole tribe of Florida. In 1832, in the Treaty of Payne's Landing, a portion of the Seminole tribe agreed to evacuate Florida as soon as suitable habitation was found in the west. Under the terms of that treaty, the tribe had three years to remove. Some did go west and settled among the Creek tribe near Ft Gibson in the Indian Territory, where they were invited to settle by the Creeks. However, a portion of the tribe resisted, led by their chief Osceola. What became known as the 'Seminole War' raged from 1835 until 1842. The protracted war was one of the costliest America had seen. Fifteen hundred American soldiers died in the fighting (mostly from disease), and the monetary cost of the war was around $20 million. For that cost, the government had succeeded in moving about 3,000 of the Seminole to the Indian Territory. Finally, in 1842, the government simply 'called off' the Seminole War. A formal peace treaty was never signed, and some Seminole proudly note that they never surrendered to the American government. A few remaining Seminole were allowed to remain in the Florida Everglades.

With the completion of the Indian Removal program, the US government believed it had permanently solved what was often called 'The Indian Problem.' The Indians had been moved west of the Mississippi, to the very western edge of US territory. Many believed that the Indians would never be molested there, because the land was not suitable for the type of agriculture that American farmers were familiar with in the east. However, this 'permanent' solution would last only a little more than twenty years. When the United States annexed Texas, and later took the rest of the southwest from Mexico, the Indian Territory was no longer on the western border of the United States, but right in the middle. In 1854, the Kansas–Nebraska Act was passed, and these areas were opened to white settlement and eventual statehood. Tribes that had been settled in what is now Kansas with the promise that these lands were theirs 'forever' were now asked to cede their lands to the government and move again, into present-day Oklahoma, which remained the 'Indian Territory' throughout the remainder of the nineteenth century.

Because of the Louisiana Purchase, Thomas Jefferson is clearly associated with American expansionism. But scholars often fail to note the extent to which his Democratic-Republican successors in the White House were also concerned with the expansion of American territory and settlement. Madison, Monroe, and John Quincy Adams were greatly concerned with the Gulf Coast region of the Old Southwest, and were intent on seeing the US claim to this land firmly established. By the end of Monroe's administration, this goal had been accomplished (Owsley and Smith, 1997: 2, 62).

In the years between the Louisiana Purchase and the annexation of Texas, the United States did not acquire any truly large blocks of territory. But expansionary policies were clearly at work. Boundary issues were settled with Great Britain and Spain, Florida was acquired, and numerous Indian tribes in the interior of the United States were dispossessed of their land and moved to the western border of the nation, where they were believed to be out of the way of the expanding white population. The fervent nationalism of the era is seen not only in these developments, but also in the issuance of the Monroe Doctrine that warned European powers to stay out of affairs in the Western Hemisphere. In short, the United States asserted not only a firm definition of its own territorial integrity, but also the existence of an American 'sphere of influence' in the Western Hemisphere in which European participation was unwelcome. By the 1830s, it was clear that the United States had 'digested' the large territory acquired in the Louisiana Purchase and in settling the matter of Florida. However, as will become clear in the following chapter, the next large acquisitions of territory would spark controversies that threatened the very existence of the nation.

CHAPTER FOUR

OREGON AND TEXAS

American expansion in the nineteenth century was not an isolated affair involving only the United States and its immediate neighbors. Instead, these expansionary moves were part of large-scale international developments that involved Great Britain, France, Spain, the independent Republic of Mexico, and Russia. The 'Oregon question' was primarily a controversy between the United States and Great Britain, but Spain and Russia also affected the claims and counter-claims made by these main disputants. Before 1819, the United States, Great Britain, Spain and Russia all laid claim to lands along the northwestern coast of the United States. By the middle of the next decade, however, the claims of Spain and Russia had been dealt with in treaties, and only the United States and Great Britain remained at odds over the region.

Likewise, the issue of the annexation of Texas was truly an international affair. After Mexico achieved its independence, Spain was no longer directly involved in this dispute. But besides the principal players – Mexico, the Republic of Texas, and the United States – other international powers were also involved in this matter, namely Great Britain and, to a lesser extent, France.

Political affairs in the United States intertwined the Texas and Oregon issues to such an extent that it becomes nearly impossible to discuss one without reference to the other. Expansionistic rhetoric by James K. Polk, during both his election campaign and his presidency, brought the United States to the brink of war with Great Britain over Oregon while another conflict loomed with Mexico over the annexation of Texas. Finally, settlement of the Oregon issue gave Polk a freer hand to move in the matters involving Mexico. This chapter will examine the Oregon controversy and its settlement, and the events leading to the annexation of Texas by the United States.

THE OREGON CONTROVERSY

As noted in the previous chapter, the Convention of 1818 settled several controversies between the United States and Great Britain over the border between the US and Canada (see Map 3). This agreement was signed in London in October 1818, and provided that the northwest boundary of the United States was set as the 49th parallel, from the Lake of the Woods (on the border of the present-day province of Ontario in Canada and the state of Minnesota in the United States) west to the crest of the Rocky Mountains. Thus, the Convention of 1818 settled the issue of the northern boundary of the Louisiana Purchase Territory. West of the Rocky Mountains, no boundary was established. The two nations agreed that people from each country could settle in the region for ten years, with the stipulation that this 'joint occupancy' would not be construed to damage the claims of either nation as to the ultimate control of the region. In 1827, the agreement was extended further in a Treaty of Joint Occupation, signed by the United States and Great Britain.

What had come to be called the 'Oregon Country' by 1840 was an expanse of approximately one-half million square miles, much of it beautiful, high quality land (see Map 4). There were excellent timber and fur resources, and one major harbor – Puget Sound – considered by many to be one of the finest natural harbors in the world. With harbors such as Puget Sound, many Americans believed the Pacific Northwest region could become a major center for trade with the Orient.

As long as the only non-Indian people in the Oregon Country were a relatively small number of fur traders, 'joint occupancy' posed few problems. But 'Oregon fever' in the early 1840s led thousands of Americans to strike out across the continent for the far west. As more and more Americans settled in Oregon and demanded the creation of a stable government, it became clear the issue had to be dealt with in a final manner. Each nation firmly asserted various claims to the Oregon Country.

The claims of the United States to the region were supported by several factors. First of all, in the Adams–Onís Treaty, Spain had relinquished its claims to this region to the United States. This treaty set the northern boundary of Spanish territory at the 42nd parallel. American diplomats considered this agreement by Spain as a tacit admission of US claims to land north of the 42nd parallel. By 1822, Tsar Alexander I of Russia had decided that Russia would no longer assert claims to any territory south of 54° 40′. This was confirmed in a treaty with the United States in 1824 and another treaty between Russia and Great Britain in 1825.

The United States also based their claims on the explorations of Captain Robert Gray in 1792. Gray sailed the *Columbia* up the mouth of the great river, which he named after his ship. The explorations of the Lewis and Clark expedition, between 1804 and 1806, were also viewed as strengthening the US claim to this territory. After the Lewis and Clark expedition, the United States government envisioned that there would eventually be a string of fur trading posts from the Upper Missouri country across the mountains to the Pacific Coast, generally along the route that Lewis and Clark had taken. The first major American fur-trading outpost in the region was Astoria, a settlement near the mouth of the Columbia River created by John Jacob Astor's American Fur Company in 1811. The American Fur Company was forced to sell Astoria to the British when the War of 1812 broke out, but the company regained the outpost in 1818, under the 'mutual-restoration' provision of the Treaty of Ghent.

American statesmen also argued that the principles of *contiguity* and *continuity* added a common-sense dimension to America's claims to the region. This argument simply affirmed that since the area is contiguous to United States territory, and would provide a continuous corridor of land across the continent, it simply ought by nature to be part of the US. The American government believed that these claims were sufficient to cement the United States' right to the Oregon territory, at least up to the 49th parallel.

Great Britain never pushed a claim for all of the Oregon Country, but wished for an equitable division with the US. British claims to the Oregon Country were based primarily on early explorations by British expeditions and on the Nootka Convention with Spain in 1790. The British explorer Captain James Cook first touched the coast of the American Northwest in 1778, which laid Britain's claim to the region. In 1792, Captain George Vancouver made further explorations in the region for the British. The Nootka Convention resulted from an affair in the Nootka Sound region in which a Spanish naval force had captured and imprisoned British fur traders in the region. After intense disputes that threatened to escalate into a general war in Europe, Spain backed down and agreed to the Nootka Convention, giving up any claims to exclusive sovereignty of the northern Pacific Coast.

The numerous fur trade outposts established there by the Hudson's Bay Company also strengthened Britain's claim to the region. By the early 1840s, the Hudson's Bay Company had approximately 3,000 employees in the Oregon Country, and the company's director functioned as the head of the government there. Thus, within sixty years of their initial claims to the region, the British had a flourishing fur trade going on in the Oregon Country (Cole, 1974: 126). Early on, because of this sizeable presence of Hudson's Bay Company operations there, the British believed that the actual occupation of the region by loyal British subjects would be sufficient to overcome the US claims. Of course, in the long run, 'Oregon Fever' in the United States meant that the region was overrun with settlers with loyalties to the US, so actual occupancy became a claim more favorable to the US position.

Despite American calls for 'All of Oregon or None!' and '54° 40' or Fight!' the entire Oregon Country was never seriously in dispute. It was generally agreed that a division between the two claimants must be made. The question was where to fix the boundary line. Great Britain expressed a willingness on several occasions to settle for a boundary along the Columbia River, for this would leave the area where the Hudson's Bay Company was dominant in trade in British hands. Likewise, the United States had several times offered to settle for the 49th parallel line simply being extended to the Pacific Coast. So what was really in dispute was the region between the Columbia River and the 49th parallel. Puget Sound with its magnificent harbor lay within this territory and was one of the reasons the Americans sought this particular area so diligently. In July of 1846, Polk confided to his diary that the United States could well agree to settle on the 49th parallel for the boundary, since this would put the principal harbors – the Straits of Fuca, Admiralty Inlet, and Puget Sound – in American hands. Relying on the testimony of travelers, Polk accepted the idea that much of the land north of the 49th parallel was unfit for agriculture and suitable chiefly for the fur trade.

The interest of the United States in Oregon cannot be divorced from the desire of American leaders for all of the Pacific Coast, with the ports that could open the door for a lucrative trade with the nations of the Pacific. American ships in the sea otter trade were plying the waters of the Pacific Coast as early as the 1790s. By the 1840s, rising American industrial production, and the belief that railroads would eventually make trans-continental transportation relatively easy, made the Pacific Coast ports all the more desirable.

'OREGON FEVER'

Perhaps unwittingly, missionaries who went to the Oregon Country to minister to the Indians were instrumental in awakening an 'Oregon fever' in the minds of many Americans. In 1831, four Nez Perce and Flathead Indians arrived in St Louis. They met with the Superintendent of Indian Affairs for the Central Superintendency, William Clark (one of the co-leaders of the Lewis and Clark expedition). The Indians asked Clark to send 'the book' and 'black robes,' meaning the Bible and Christian missionaries. Their request was perceived as a 'Macedonian call' by many American churches, and sparked a renewed interest in Indian missions.

Jason Lee, a Methodist minister, was one of the first missionaries to go to Oregon, arriving in 1834. Two Presbyterian missionary families under the auspices of the American Board of Commissioners for Foreign Missions later joined him, Marcus and Narcissa Whitman and Henry and Eliza Spalding. Narcissa Whitman and Eliza Spalding were probably the first women to make a transcontinental journey across North America. When the missionaries wrote back to their families, friends, and supporters, their reports of the beauty and richness of the Oregon Country, especially the Willamette valley, sparked the interest of settlers.

By 1841, 'Oregon fever' was affecting many in the northern states. Lured by these reports of the beautiful rich lands, perhaps as many as 10,000 went overland to the northwest in the next five years. In jumping off points like Independence and Westport, Missouri, they formed wagon trains and set out for a six-month journey across 2,000 miles. The travelers had a short window of opportunity for leaving their eastern jumping-off points: they had to wait late enough in the spring to have new grass for their livestock along the way. But if they waited too long before departing, they could be caught in the mountains when winter hit.

In the south, annexation of Oregon was seen as a golden opportunity. Many believed that if the Oregon country could be brought into the Union as free territory, then opposition to annexing Texas would diminish. When the treaty for the annexation of Texas was rejected in 1844, many southern politicians became more pessimistic, and worried that the south might no longer be able to control its own destiny in Congress.

With both Oregon and Texas on the minds of politicians and voters in 1844, expansionism became a major issue in that year's election. The Democrats nominated Speaker of the House, James K. Polk. One of the reasons they bypassed the preconvention favorite, Martin Van Buren, was because his antislavery sentiments had led him to oppose annexation of Texas. John Tyler, who had succeeded to the presidency when William Henry Harrison died after less than a month in office, had alienated much of his own party, so was never seriously considered for re-nomination by the Whigs. Instead, the Whigs turned to Henry Clay, who made his third unsuccessful run for the presidency.

Both Polk and Clay spoke in favor of expansion during the campaign in 1844. However, Clay played upon fears that the rash policies advocated by the Democrats might provoke a war with Britain. Instead, he called for negotiations and more careful expansionary moves. Polk spoke out more blatantly for expansion, calling for the 'reannexation' of Texas, and the 'reoccupation' of Oregon, implying that the United States had prior claims to both of these disputed regions. Polk won a very narrow victory, carrying 15 of the 26 states, winning 170 electoral college votes to Clay's 105. In the popular vote, the margin of victory was only 38,000 out of a total of 2.7 million votes cast. Historian Ray Allen Billington noted, 'As is so often the case, the truth was less important than the impression created by Polk's victory. Both he and the nation believed that the people had spoken for expansion, no matter what the cost' (Billington, 1956: 144). While Polk did not really have anything like a mandate from the people, the Whig party believed that expansionism and especially the Texas question had been keys to Polk's victory.

SETTLEMENT OF THE OREGON CRISIS

In his inaugural address, Polk challenged the British: 'Our title to the country of the Oregon [*sic*] is clear and unquestionable, and already are our people preparing to perfect that title by occupying it with their wives and children' (quoted in Billington, 1956: 155). Despite this public rhetoric Polk, now facing the increasing likelihood of war with Mexico, held out an olive branch to the British: he would agree to the 49th parallel boundary because previous presidents had made that offer. This time the British disagreed. In fact, the British minister in Washington flatly refused the offer and failed to inform London of it.

The influx of American settlers played a decisive role in the outcome of the situation in Oregon. As noted earlier, one of the reasons that the British were much interested in the area along the Columbia River was because of the operations of the Hudson's Bay Company in that region. The Company had built a small but thriving colony there, of about 750 British subjects. There were over 5,000 American settlers in Oregon, but all of them were in the Willamette Valley. Hudson's Bay Company officials had encouraged the Americans to settle south of the Columbia, so the American settlers were not in the area that was in dispute. But the British did not want to give up the Hudson's Bay Company's operations in the region, and the matter might have been much harder to settle if the Company had not expressed a change of heart. The coming of the Americans had meant a displacement of the fur-bearing animals, and the operations of the Hudson's Bay Company had been shifting northward for some time. In 1840 the Company built a trading post at Ft Victoria on Vancouver Island, in case Ft Vancouver (on the mainland) had to be abandoned in the future. In January 1845, the company shifted their operations to the new fort, and informed the British government they would not object to a settlement at the 49th parallel.

Polk blustered in public about taking all of the Oregon country, but in private his emissaries worked out a sensible treaty with Great Britain, by which the territory was to be divided by simply extending the 49th parallel boundary further westward. The Senate ratified the Oregon Treaty in June 1846. Thus, after many rounds of negotiations, an agreement was reached on a proposed settlement line that had been previously offered by both sides on numerous occasions (see Map 4).

THE AMERICAN SOUTHWEST

Settling the Oregon issue with Great Britain allowed Polk to turn his attention more fully to the Texas question. Polk believed that annexation of Texas could become a prelude to US expansion all the way across the southwest to the Pacific Coast (see Map 5). Polk was particularly interested in Alta California and the superb harbor at San Francisco. Thus, while it was ostensibly border issues along the disputed boundary between Texas and Mexico that brought on the US–Mexican War, Polk made it clear from the beginning that the settlement of the war would also involve US acquisition of California and New Mexico.

Texas was a long-standing object of the desires of expansionistic Americans. Some American statesmen had long argued that at least the eastern parts of Texas had been part of the Louisiana Purchase. However, Spanish officials interpreted the Adams–Onís Treaty of 1819 as ending any American claim to Texas. The United States had made efforts to purchase Texas from Mexico as early as 1825, during the administration of President John Quincy Adams. Andrew Jackson had envisioned annexing all of Spanish America, and also attempted to purchase Texas from Mexico. While he balked on the annexation of Texas when the opportunity first appeared, Jackson clearly wanted to acquire Texas if it could be done without risking a war with Mexico or creating a sectional crisis in the United States.

Well before any official US government action was undertaken, American filibusters attempted to foment trouble in Texas, hoping that unsettled conditions might lead to American annexation. This filibustering activity involved both invaders from outside and Americans who had actually settled in Texas. American settlers had been squatting illegally on Spanish lands in Texas since early in the nineteenth century, with scattered farms in the area around Nagadoches and along the south bank of the Red River. Filibustering activity against the Spanish in Texas increased after 1815, but the US government did not formally back or coordinate any of these efforts.

In the early nineteenth century, as revolutionary fervor swept South and Central America and the Spanish empire began to crumble, the Spanish struggled to hold on to Mexico. There were attempts among Mexicans to push for independence as early as 1810, but the revolution was not successful until 1821. Under the Spanish, Mexican society was dominated by a small number of *criollos* – people of Spanish blood who had been born in the New World. Under them, the bulk of Mexican society was made up of Indians and *mestizos* – people of mixed Spanish and Indian heritage. In 1821, Agustín de Iturbide, a conservative member of the *criollo* class, succeeded in uniting the opposition to Spanish rule and achieved Mexican independence. Iturbide established an empire and ruled as 'Emperor,' but struggles continued in Mexico over what kind of government the nation should have. Eventually, in 1823, Iturbide was deposed and a republic was established in Mexico.

AMERICAN SETTLERS IN TEXAS

Texas was on the extreme northern fringe of the Spanish New World empire, and the Spanish had been relatively late in making any significant efforts at colonizing the region. At the time of Mexican independence, only some 2,500 Spanish-speaking settlers lived in the vast expanse of Texas, and about half of these lived in and around San Antonio, the provincial capital. In the years immediately preceding Mexican independence, Spanish officials had begun to encourage settlement in Texas by making generous land grants available. They hoped that a settled Texas would be a barrier to Indian raiders and a block to further American expansionism. Believing that settlers from the United States (and elsewhere) could be converted into loyal citizens of the Spanish empire, they negotiated with Moses Austin to bring in 300 Catholic families to colonize Texas. In return, Austin was given a huge grant of land along the Brazos River. However, before Moses Austin could begin his colony, the Spanish lost control of Mexico as a result of the Mexican Revolution.

The United States showed considerable interest in Mexican independence. American statesmen believed that an independent Mexico would weaken Spain, making future expansionary moves by the US easier. The decline of the Spanish empire in the New World could also open more opportunities for American trade with Latin American nations. Both the United States and Great Britain showed greater interest in Mexico after the young nation achieved independence from Spain. Britain was interested in Mexican markets for its industrial output, and in some raw materials in that region as well. They also desired to see Mexico provide a barrier to the further southwestern expansion of the United States. The United States was the first foreign nation to recognize the new Republic of Mexico, and, immediately after the Mexican revolution, relations between the United States and Mexico were generally cordial.

In 1824, Mexico adopted a federal constitution that created the office of President, a representative Congress and a judicial system that were all modeled on the United States' system. The Constitution guaranteed many of the rights of Mexican citizens. Freedom of religion was an exception, as only Catholicism was allowed. Under this new federal constitution, the new state of Coahuila y Texas was created, and the capital was moved from San Antonio to Saltillo.

After Mexico gained its independence, the new government realized the need for more settlement and development in the region, so it continued colonization policies similar to those the Spanish government had instituted. Moses Austin had died shortly after getting his original grant from the Spanish, but his son Stephen F. Austin eventually secured an agreement from the Mexican government to allow the colonization scheme to go forward. Settlers from anywhere were welcomed. While a few did come from Europe, most of the people who took advantage of the generous grants of land were citizens of the United States. The Mexican Colonization Law of 1824 granted sizeable land holdings, and promised security and exemption from taxes for four years to all settlers. Foreign settlers were forbidden to settle along the international border, or along the seacoast – indicating that there may have been some doubt among Mexican officials about the ultimate loyalty of some potential settlers. Yet, by giving them land and a stake in the future of the country, the Mexican republic hoped eventually to secure the loyalty of these settlers. Before this Colonization Law was adopted, there were already about 3,000 Americans illegally squatting on Mexican land in Texas.

The terms offered to these settlers were very generous. In the state of Coahuila y Texas, foreign colonists could receive 4,428 acres of land for grazing livestock and 170 acres of land suitable for cultivation. In return, they had to pay a modest fee, but had six years to complete payment. Officially, these settlers were supposed to be 'Roman Apostolic Catholics, and of steady habits' (quoted in Christiansen and Christiansen, 1998: 16).

Empresarios who had been given large tracts of land to use in settling colonists became middlemen between the Mexican government and the settlers. Stephen Austin became the most successful of the *empresarios*. In addition to the 300 families that his father's original contact had authorized, Austin received permission to settle an additional 900 families.

Settlers who took up these lands were required to become Mexican citizens. Since the Roman Catholic Church was the officially established religion in Mexico, these new settlers were supposedly required to convert to Catholicism. This requirement seems to have been lightly enforced, as only an estimated 10 percent of the colonists ever converted to Catholicism. While settlers were generally not forced to convert, the government did prohibit any other form of public worship, and many settlers resented this restriction.

A new constitution adopted for the state of Coahuila y Texas in 1827 provided for a gradual emancipation of all slaves in the region. In 1829, slavery was abolished throughout all of Mexico by presidential decree, although Texas was exempted from this decree by later actions that same year. Since many of the Americans who had come into Texas were originally from the American South, many had brought slaves with them.

By 1830, there were approximately 7,000 American settlers living in

Texas. They outnumbered the native *tejanos* in the region by more than two to one. Most of these American settlers had taken up land in eastern and central Texas, and remained isolated from the native Mexican settlements farther to the southwest, such as Goliad and San Antonio. Texas was separated from the heart of Mexico by hundreds of miles of rough, empty country, trade with the United States was much easier than trade with the Mexican interior, and the hopes of the Mexican government to tie these colonists to Mexico were not realized. The American settlers in Texas, while settled on the lands of a foreign nation, were actually an isolated American colony with little connection to the people or the government of Mexico. Many Mexican officials also feared the pro-American tendencies of the Texas settlers, and the acquisitiveness of the United States.

Eventually, Mexico tried to counter the foreign influence of these American settlers by assigning more soldiers to garrisons in Texas and encouraging more native Mexican citizens to move into the region. Few Mexican settlers went: the wealthy had no incentive to go, the poor could not afford to go and set up farms or ranches, even if the land was given to them. New laws passed in April 1830 blocked further emigration from America. These laws also cancelled the *empresario* contracts then in effect, and outlawed slavery in Texas. Slavery had been outlawed in Mexico the previous year, but the law had generally not been enforced and slaves in Texas were considered to be in a form of indentured servitude. Neither the antislavery law nor the prohibition of new settlement was effectively enforced, but the Texas settlers feared that the authorities might eventually crack down. Despite the changes in the law, illegal entry into Texas by American settlers actually increased, and many of these settlers brought more slaves with them. More Mexican soldiers were garrisoned in Texas, but the government was not successful in encouraging Mexican citizens to move to the region to counter the growing American presence. By 1835, the American population in Texas was about 30,000, and about 3,000 black slaves were also there. American settlers outnumbered the Spanish-speaking settlers in Texas by more than ten to one.

THE REPUBLIC OF TEXAS

The Texas Revolution was not simply a revolt of American settlers in Texas against Mexican rule. Traditionally, historians have seen the origins of the Texas Revolution in the cultural or ethnic incompatibility between Mexicans and the American settlers. However, even native-born *tejanos* (Mexican citizens born in the province of Texas) had reason to resent the centralizing power of the Mexican politician and dictator Antonio Lopez de Santa Anna. In fact, the first impulse to organize local militias to resist the power of the central government came in the *tejano* settlements in Coahuila and the San Antonio–Goliad regions. Thus, trade ties, ethnic relations, the political situation in Mexico, and international affairs concerning the United States, Great Britain, France and Spain complicated the situation in Texas.

As soon as Mexico became independent of Spain, business interests in the United States and several European nations began to pursue economic contacts that created many ties between Mexico and these various nations. While Mexican and European investors were interested in lands in Texas and New Mexico, it was United States citizens that showed the greatest interest in these areas. American speculators believed that an independent Texas, or Texas annexed into the Union, would cause land values to rise dramatically, so there was great interest in the potential profits that might result. Besides the general investment potential of land for agricultural pursuits and town site development, there was also great interest in the Gulf Coast region as possible sites for ports for the sea-borne trade.

Economic interests that bound Texans – both settlers and native *tejanos* – to the United States were an important factor leading to the Texas Revolution. Historian Andres Resendez has noted that those who profited from trade ties tended to shift their political allegiance in ways that accommodated their economic interests. These shifting alliances involved not only Anglo settlers, but *tejanos* and American Indians as well. Spanish imperial policy had prohibited or strictly limited trade between the northern Mexican provinces and the United States, but Mexican independence removed many of these barriers. Fearing that the northern provinces might be enticed into the embrace of the United States, the Mexican government undertook to build a sense of nationalism in this region through schools, newspapers and other printed literature, and public ceremonies full of nationalistic ritual. None of this seemed to cement the loyalties of the people in the region to the central government. Economic change, which created ties across ethnic and national lines, overpowered these efforts at building nationalism (Resendez, 1999: 669, 674–8).

Texas settlers resented the laws passed by the Mexican Congress in April 1830, restricting further American immigration and outlawing slavery. Some Texan leaders were ready to move for independence from Mexico. However, Stephen Austin hoped to avoid warfare and went to Mexico City to present Texan grievances to Santa Anna. While there he was arrested and imprisoned for eight months. Coming back to Texas after his release, Austin was now ready to join those calling for independence.

By the 1830s, Mexican politics was divided into two broad camps: liberals who wanted a more republican form of government, a weakening of the military, and a lessening of the official power and influence of the Roman Catholic Church in Mexico. Because they supported a federal system of government, with some power left in the hands of state governments, this party was sometimes called the Federalists. Geographically, the regions distant from Mexico City, including the border areas, were generally aligned with the Federalists. Opposing them were the Centrists, who wanted a unified national government, with most power directed from Mexico City. Many of the Centrists were also generally conservative, and opposed most reformist ideas. These Centrists tended to see anyone who advocated local or regional autonomy within the Mexican state as separatists.

It would be nearly impossible to overstate the significance of Santa Anna in Mexican history, from the time of independence from Spain until the mid-1840s. Noting that Santa Anna is reviled by many, historian John S. D. Eisenhower suggests that 'it would be difficult to find a man who could have better represented his country than he did, given the state of confusion and poverty besetting that unhappy land at that time.' Eisenhower goes on to surmise, 'He was, with all his faults, the best leader Mexico could produce at that time' (Eisenhower, 1989: 8–9). In 1832, Santa Anna defeated the army of the conservative Centrist government, and new elections were scheduled for January 1833. In those elections, Santa Anna was elected president of the Republic of Mexico but he did not immediately take office. Citing health concerns, he allowed his vice-president to govern for a time. However, within six weeks much of the conservative faction in Mexico had been alienated by some mild attempts at reform. The acting president was forced to step down and Santa Anna took office, appearing to have saved Mexico from anarchy once again.

By December 1834, Santa Anna had succeeded in acquiring dictatorial powers in Mexico. Many Federalists or liberals throughout Mexico, along with the settlers living in Texas, considered that a revolution against him, aimed at restoring the principles of the Constitution of 1824, might be a necessary step. Citizens in areas such as Texas, which had enjoyed a good deal of self-government under earlier Mexican rulers, were especially concerned about the centralizing powers that Santa Anna claimed. However, Federalists in Mexico, while they sympathized with the Texans, warned that an attempt to push for Texas independence would unite all of Mexico against the Texan.

Santa Anna moved to consolidate his power, repudiating the Federalist principles upon which he had based his move toward the presidency. He adopted the Centrist position that argued for absolute rule by the central government over all Mexicans, including the settlers in Texas.

Violent opposition to these policies broke out in Texas. At town meetings throughout Texas in August 1835, a call was extended for a general meeting for representatives' from all of Texas. This meeting was to begin on 15 October 1835, in Washington-on-the-Brazos. However, because of disturbances throughout the region that fall, the meeting did not take place until early November. Even before this convention met, those calling for war and aiming for full independence for Texas were spreading propaganda and appealing for aid in the United States.

Skirmishing between Texans and Mexican forces began even before the convention met at Washington-on-the-Brazos. Demands that the village of Gonzales return a cannon that had been loaned to them for defense against Indian attacks were met with violent opposition. On 2 October 1835 a force of 100 Mexican dragoons rode to the village to retrieve the cannon. Approximately 160 volunteer militiamen from Gonzales and neighboring villages gathered to confront them. After a brief skirmish the dragoons were forced to retreat. News of the skirmish at Gonzales spread rapidly, and volunteers from throughout Texas, and some from the United States, began streaming toward Gonzales. A week later a force of about 125 Texas volunteers captured the presidio at Goliad, overpowering the Mexican garrison of approximately 40 men.

When the meetings at Washington-on-the-Brazos began on 1 November 1835, two parties quickly emerged: one faction called for a war for total independence from Mexico, the other called for armed resistance only in order to force compliance with the liberal provisions of the Mexican Constitution of 1824. The meeting continued until 13 November, and the Texan representatives finally voted to endorse the position of the Mexican Federalists, opposing the centralization of power under Santa Anna. Many who believed independence would be the ultimate end of the matter may well have voted for the less drastic position at this point. Time was needed to raise an army and the funds to fight a war. Standing for liberal ideals against a despotic ruler might also gain more sympathy from the United States. Furthermore, siding with the Mexican Federalists might further divide the political factions in Mexico, which could be desirable if a move toward independence was undertaken later. The convention also made plans to raise an army to resist Santa Anna, and named representatives to be sent to the United States to solicit aid.

In December 1835 Santa Anna established a unitary state that denied all local rights throughout Mexican territory. He also put together an army of 6,000 men to march to Texas and deal with the opposition of the settlers there. In response to this, Texans held a second convention at Washington-on-the-Brazos in early March 1836. On 2 March they approved a declaration of independence and drew up a constitution very similar to the US Constitution to govern the new Republic of Texas. On 4 March Sam Houston was named commander of the army of the new republic.

Forces raised to fight for independence were already occupying an abandoned mission at San Antonio known as the Alamo. In late February, Santa Anna had begun a siege of the Alamo, with an army of 3,000 men. In a classic stand-off that has become legendary in Texas history, 187 Texans refused demands to surrender and held out until 6 March. On that date, Santa Anna's forces stormed the Alamo and killed all of the defenders. Outraged Texans and their supporters in the United States took up the cry of 'Remember the Alamo,' and vowed vengeance against Santa Anna. An even more brutal incident followed just three weeks later at Goliad, where approximately 340 defenders surrendered after being promised just treatment by the Mexican forces. After being led out of their defensive position, the prisoners of war were slaughtered by the Mexican troops. The siege of the Alamo, and the atrocity committed at Goliad, provoked loud outcries throughout Texas and in the American press. Officially, the United States remained neutral, but many American volunteers went to Texas to help in the fighting.

Victories in one skirmish after another followed for Santa Anna and his troops. By the middle of April 1836 the Mexican forces had pushed through Southern Texas all the way to Galveston Bay, with Texan forces and refugees fleeing before them. However, just as victory seemed within his grasp, Santa Anna was defeated and captured at the Battle of San Jacinto, near Galveston Bay, on 21 April 1836. The Texan army under Sam Houston, with about 800 soldiers, surprised the much larger Mexican force during their afternoon siesta. Outraged at what had happened at the Alamo and Goliad, the Texans killed many Mexican soldiers who were trying to surrender. Altogether, about 630 Mexican troops were killed, about 200 wounded, and over 700 captured at San Jacinto.

Santa Anna attempted to escape dressed in the uniform of a common soldier. When he was captured, many of the Texans wanted to execute him, but Sam Houston ordered that he be protected. The victorious Texans forced Santa Anna to agree to two treaties, one that was an official public treaty and a second that was secret. The official treaty provided that the war was over, that prisoners of war would be exchanged, that Texans would be recompensed for property destroyed in the fighting, and that the Mexican army was to remain south of the Rio Grande. The secret treaty went further to promise Santa Anna his freedom in return for assurance that Mexico would officially recognize the independence of Texas, and would accept the Rio Grande as the southern boundary of the independent republic.

As soon as news of Santa Anna's defeat and capture reached Mexico City, his opponents moved to take over the government. Anastacio Bustamente declared himself acting president of Mexico, and on 20 May 1836, he formally revoked any treaties concluded by Santa Anna. In fact, Bustamente intended to gather forces to continue the war, although hostilities did not break out again.

While the authorities of the newly established government in Mexico disavowed the treaty which Santa Anna had signed granting Texas its independence, foreign nations generally recognized it. Shortly after Texas declared independence, the US Senate had extended formal recognition of the new republic. Agents of the Texan government were in Washington, DC, by the end of 1835, trying to secure recognition by the US. The US Congress had already instructed President Jackson to send an agent to Texas to report on the situation there. While US recognition of the Republic of Texas was swift, other nations were slower to respond. Great Britain was reluctant to show support for a revolution in Texas while they feared the possibility of the same thing happening in Canada. There were also business interests at stake, for lands in the northern provinces secured Mexican debts to some British interests. However, Great Britain did extend recognition to the Republic of Texas in 1841. France was also reluctant to recognize the new republic because they doubted the ability of the Texans to maintain their sovereignty, but eventually they did sign a commercial treaty with the Republic of Texas in September 1839.

Texas had won its independence from Mexico, but in doing so it had exhausted its financial resources. The army that had defeated Santa Anna needed to be paid, and crops needed to be sown for the summer growing season. In many places, farms and ranches had been destroyed as fleeing Texans had destroyed everything rather than leave it for Santa Anna's troops.

The US government never officially intervened in the struggle between Texas and Mexico. However, public opinion in the United States was firmly on the side of the Texas rebels. The greatest enthusiasm came from the region south of the Ohio River. People sympathetic to the Texans' struggle raised money and recruited volunteers to fight for Texas, but because of the swiftness of the Texans' victory over Santa Anna, most of the aid that was sent by American citizens arrived after Texas had already won its independence.

However important American aid and volunteers may actually have been to the Texans, Mexicans tended to believe that US aid had provided the margin of victory, and thus US–Mexican relations were embittered even before the annexation of Texas. Before the Texas Revolution, many Mexicans had viewed the United States positively, and believed that their own nation would benefit from imitating many American institutions. But US support of the Texans changed this, and many Mexicans came to distrust the United States; Mexican politicians endangered their own careers if they took any stance that might seem to be conciliatory toward the United States.

THE ANNEXATION OF TEXAS

Soon after gaining independence from Mexico, Texas petitioned for admission into the United States. In elections in September 1836, Sam Houston was elected president of the Republic of Texas, and Mirabeau Lamar was made vice-president. In a referendum that was part of the election, the majority of Texan voters declared themselves in favor of annexation to the United States. Most Texans generally assumed that the United States would rapidly take up their request and add the new territory to the nation. However, the question of expansion into the southwest prompted the renewal of the old sectional debate. Slavery had existed illegally in Texas while it was a part of Mexico, and the Republic of Texas had allowed slavery after winning its independence. Thus, it was virtually certain that the admission of Texas would mean adding a new and very large slave state to the nation.

Andrew Jackson and his successor Martin Van Buren sought to avoid dealing with the question. While Jackson had moved quickly to recognize the independence of Texas, he urged caution on going any further. In one of his last messages to Congress in December 1836, he urged delay in dealing with the matter of Texas 'lest the world suspect the United States of annexationist intentions' (quoted in Pletcher, 1973: 73). When Martin Van Buren was inaugurated as president of the United States in March 1837, he did not desire to go further with the matter. As vice-president under Andrew Jackson in the immediately preceding administration, Van Buren had been reluctant even to grant recognition. Economic troubles at home preoccupied Van Buren, and he was unwilling to risk the unity of the Democratic Party and the adoption of his economic measures by making a strong case for the annexation of Texas.

The Whig party opposed annexation because they believed it symbolized virtually everything they disagreed upon with their Democratic opponents. The Whigs charged that taking on such a large territory at once was dangerous. Since it would benefit slaveholders, it was also anti-republican. Some of the Whigs believed that the republic could not endure if it became too large, and they argued for a more restrained policy of expansion. Thus they argued that the annexation of Texas could lead to fragmentation and anarchy. Southern Whigs also believed that adding Texas as a slave state would cause a rapid exodus of slaveholders from older areas of the south, leaving behind ruined lands. After some initial flurries of activity and interest, the Texas issue remained relatively quiet until the spring of 1843. Differences over annexation between the two major political parties and between the sections kept the issue in the background.

President John Tyler enthusiastically embraced the cause of annexation.

A former Democrat, he had broken with Andrew Jackson on the issue of the national bank controversy. He became a Whig and was put on the ballot as vice-president under William Henry Harrison. When Harrison died after less than a month in office Tyler succeeded to the presidency. As president, the Whig party believed that Tyler reverted to some of his old Democratic ideals. He regularly vetoed Whig bills for internal improvements at national expense. As it became increasingly clear that he could expect no Whig support for an attempt at re-election in 1844, Tyler began to push expansionism as an issue he believed might draw support. However, in a vote split by sections, the Senate failed to ratify an 1844 treaty for annexation. While Texas had initially wanted a swift annexation to the United States, after this rebuff there was a change in sentiment in Texas and enthusiasm for annexation declined. Feeling like a rejected suitor, the administration of Texas President Lamar opposed any renewal of the annexation offer for some time. Yet, while the enthusiasm of the Texas government cooled, trade ties between the United States and the Republic of Texas continued to grow: American investors were speculating in lands, and New Orleans was developing a brisk trade.

Fear of British influence in the region was a factor in changing American attitudes about annexation. According to this interpretation, when Texan leaders began openly discussing the possibilities of seeking ties and perhaps alliances with Great Britain, this seemed to push many Americans toward believing the annexation of Texas was a necessity. However, a rumor was circulating as early as 1837 that Great Britain was trying to purchase Texas, but this did not move Van Buren to change his opposition to annexation.

Congress debated the issue heatedly, with extension of slavery the major question. An important argument used by those who favored annexation was that it was merely a case of reuniting former Americans, who wished to be annexed, with their original homeland.

In his last days in office, Tyler proposed Texas be admitted as a state through a joint resolution of Congress, rather than by treaty. The House of Representatives approved a resolution for the annexation of Texas on 25 January 1845. The vote in the House was 120 to 98. Initially, the Senate was reluctant to go along with this procedure, for fear that it might infringe on the Senate's constitutionally mandated power to ratify treaties. Finally, the Senate agreed to a resolution that stated that the offer of annexation could be forwarded to Texas by the president, if he felt that a formal treaty was not needed. The Senate passed the joint resolution on 27 February 1845 by a vote of 27 to 25 – a bare majority, far less than the two-thirds vote that would have been required to ratify a formal treaty. Since it was less than two weeks before Polk was to be inaugurated, most of those in the Senate who voted for the resolution assumed that the decision on passing the matter on to Texas would be made by the new president. But three days before Tyler left office, he signed the measure and sent an agent to Texas to formalize the arrangements for annexation. Mexico, as it had long threatened, responded by breaking diplomatic relations with the United States. Many believed war was imminent.

When the United States offered statehood to Texas, the Mexican government under President José Joaquin de Herrera offered to recognize the independence of Texas if the Texans would rebuff annexation. But the people of Texas voted in a referendum in July 1845 to become part of the United States.

Even at this point, there was some cause to believe that Mexican opposition to annexation might be dropped if the border issue could be settled. While Texas was a Mexican province, the government of Mexico considered its western boundary to be the Nueces River. But Texas had claimed everything to the Rio Grande which included not only a buffer zone between the two rivers in South Texas, but also included land far to the north, into what is now the states of New Mexico and Colorado, along the drainage of the Rio Grande River (see Map 5). The joint resolution that Congress had passed provided that the final boundary would be subject to negotiations between the president and the Republic of Mexico.

The annexation of Texas was the most immediate of the causes of the war that broke out between Mexico and the United States in 1846, but it was not the only one. Both nations were brought to the point of war by misunderstandings among their political leaders. Mexican officials feared the voracious appetite of the United States for the lands of its neighbors, and could not believe that American acquisitiveness would suddenly stop at the banks of the Rio Grande. Politicians in the United States could not understand the reluctance of Mexico to sell lands that were largely unsettled and likely to remain so for some time. The political climate in Mexico was such that any Mexican politician who seemed to even entertain the notion of negotiating a sale of territory to the United States endangered his own career. At the same time, political leaders in the United States came to believe they had a mandate from their people for rapid territorial expansion. James K. Polk had threatened to go to war with both Mexico and Great Britain, if necessary, to acquire Oregon and Texas. With the Oregon issue settled, he moved with firm resolve to come to terms with Mexico over the American southwest. He preferred a peaceful, negotiated purchase, but if that proved impossible, certainly some excuse could be found for a war that would provide a justification for annexation of further Mexican territory.

CHAPTER FIVE

THE WAR WITH MEXICO

Until recently, American scholars have not given the Mexican War the attention it deserves. There are several reasons for this. One is that the significance of the Mexican War is often eclipsed by the American Civil War, a more cataclysmic conflict which began just fifteen years later (Eisenhower, 1989: xvii). The story of the Mexican War often gets lost in the discussion of the myriad of factors leading to the Civil War. Another reason that American historians have failed to devote enough attention to the Mexican War is that the story of America's role in this conflict is in many ways a sordid one. When Americans do discuss the Mexican War, a question that quickly arises is how and why the war started. Was the United States justified in going to war against Mexico in 1846? Ulysses Grant wrote bluntly in his memoirs of his conviction that the Mexican War had been unjust (Grant, 1999: 26–7). In recent years, the trend of historiographic interpretations has tended to agree with Grant's assessment. But this has not always been the case. In a scholarly two-volume history entitled *The War With Mexico*, published in 1919, historian Justin H. Smith argued that Mexico was to blame for the outbreak of the war. Smith believed that Mexico wanted the war, threatened hostilities against the United States, and issued orders to commanders to initiate the fighting (Eisenhower, 1989: xvii; cf. Brack, 1975: 8–9). In recent years, Mexican historians, while not abandoning the concept of US aggression as the major factor in bringing on the war, have nevertheless recognized that there was a considerable pro-war faction in Mexico that bears some responsibility for the conflict.

The Mexican War led to the United States annexing large parts of northern Mexico as 'spoils of war.' However, several US presidents in succession had tried peacefully to negotiate a purchase of portions of these lands, especially Texas, New Mexico, and California. Neither side seemed capable of understanding the other in these attempts. The United States could not see why Mexico would not accept reasonable offers for lands that were largely unsettled and likely to remain so indefinitely under Mexican control. On the other hand, the Mexicans noted that while the US offered to make purchases, there were always American settlers and filibusterers lurking around the lands in question, which seemed to threaten that the territory might simply be taken if a sale could not be arranged. Thus, Mexican politicians were suspicious of American motives, especially in light of the rapid growth the United States had experienced since its independence.

ORIGINS OF THE WAR

The United States' annexation of Texas was an important immediate cause of the Mexican War, but not the only one. While relations had generally been good between the United States and Mexico immediately after Mexican independence, the ever-present fear of American expansionist desires quickly poisoned these relations. Diplomatic efforts to settle these troubles had little prospect of success: the United States was unlikely to give up attempts to purchase Mexican land, and public opinion in Mexico made it virtually impossible for any Mexican politician to even publicly suggest the sale of land to the northern neighbor. Another serious issue between the two nations was the claims made by American citizens for damages against the Mexican government. Mexico had acknowledged the validity of these claims but could not pay them. Political instability within the Mexican republic exacerbated all of these problems. For example, on the one hand, there was a monarchist faction in Mexico which hoped that war with the United States would so debilitate Mexico that the situation would demand a return to monarchy. On the other extreme, the *puros* faction wanted far-reaching republican reforms. In fact, at the end of the war the *puros* wished the war to continue so that the power and privileges of both the army and the Roman Catholic Church might be destroyed.

In the summer of 1844, the Senate had rejected a treaty of annexation in a close vote that broke along sectional lines. In the 'lame duck' days of his administration (after the election of November 1844), President John Tyler began to push for the annexation of Texas, even though the Mexican President Santa Anna had formally warned the US a year earlier that annexation of Texas would be viewed as virtually a declaration of war. Tyler interpreted James K. Polk's election in November 1844 as a mandate from the people favoring expansion.

In late 1844, José Joaquín de Herrera was named provisional president of Mexico after Santa Anna had been deposed in a revolution. Herrera offered to recognize the independence of Texas, if the United States would remove warships from the coast of Mexico. However, even appearing ready to discuss such matters hurt Herrera politically. There was a large pro-war faction in the Mexican press and political community, and some Mexican politicians argued that the nation had to fight to preserve its territorial integrity, and to teach the United States a lesson.

Since the 1844 Texas annexation treaty had failed to receive the two-thirds approval in the Senate necessary for ratification, Tyler proposed that Congress consider annexing Texas by a joint resolution of both the House and the Senate. A joint resolution would require only a simple majority in both houses for passage. Both houses of Congress debated the issue heatedly in the early days of 1845, with the extension of slavery being the major question. Finally, the joint resolution was passed in late February, and three days before Tyler left office, he signed the measure. Mexico responded by breaking diplomatic relations with the United States. In a short time, both nations had moved troops to the disputed territory.

In his 1844 presidential campaign, Polk had campaigned on a strong platform calling for expansion into both Texas and the Oregon country. But as he took office, with the possibility of war looming with Mexico, Polk agreed to a negotiated settlement with Britain over the Oregon question. Thus he avoided the possibility that the United States might have to fight Great Britain and Mexico at the same time. Polk used Mexico's refusal to negotiate over Texas and potential sales of other territory as a justification for sending troops to the disputed area.

While it was the annexation of Texas into the United States that brought on the crisis with Mexico, President Polk made it clear that California and New Mexico would also be involved in any settlement with Mexico (see Map 5). California had long been of interest to American statesmen, mariners and businessmen. As early as Andrew Jackson's administration, the United States had made attempts to purchase California, but Mexico refused all suggestions to negotiate the matter.

Few American settlers had gone to California until the late 1830s, although traders sailing along the coast had been involved in the fur trade and in the cattle hide trade. In 1844, President Tyler sent John C. Frémont on an expedition to survey the Great Basin area in what is now Utah and some of the adjoining states. Frémont made accurate surveys of regions that had not been mapped before, and eventually traveled into the Sacramento River valley in California. His favorable descriptions of the area brought California to the notice of many Americans. Settlers who went to California believed it to be a paradise. They reported that the land could produce virtually any important crop grown in the world – grains, hemp, flax, cotton, tobacco, fruits and nuts. Besides the obvious attractions for agriculture, California was also important as a jumping-off point for trade to the Pacific.

While he was willing to give up the more extreme claims in the case of Oregon, Polk held firm in regard to Texas and the southwest. Polk told his cabinet that the acquisition of California – with the ports at San Diego and San Francisco – was the primary goal of his presidency. On the day of his inauguration, he told his Secretary of the Navy George Bancroft that the four great measures he hoped to accomplish were: reduction of the tariff, the re-establishment of the independent treasury, the settlement of the Oregon question, and the acquisition of California.

In the summer of 1845 President Polk ordered Zachary Taylor to move American troops into Texas, ostensibly to guard against possible attacks from Mexico after the annexation of Texas became official. He may have hoped that this show of force would bring the Mexicans to accept negotiations over the Texas border and potential sales in other regions. By the end of July 1845, Taylor had established a base camp near Corpus Christi, Texas. By the end of that year, he was commanding approximately 4,000 men, roughly half of the entire US Army.

In the fall of 1845 Polk learned that Mexico might be willing to re-establish diplomatic relations. He then sent John L. Slidell to Mexico City with instructions to negotiate a settlement on the Texas border issue, and to tender an offer to purchase upper California and New Mexico. Before sending Slidell, he told his cabinet of what he wished to accomplish through the negotiations he hoped to instigate: 'One great object of the Mission, as stated by the President, would be to adjust a permanent Boundary between Mexico and the U. States, and that in doing this the minister would be instructed to purchase for a pecuniary consideration Upper California and New Mexico.' Polk, writing in the third person in his diary, went on to record 'The President said that for such a boundary the am[oun]t of pecuniary consideration to be paid would be of small importance. He supposed it might be had for fifteen or twenty millions, but he was ready to pay forty millions for it, if it could not be had for less' (Polk's diary, quoted in McCoy, 1960: 95).

Slidell learned that while the Mexicans would not publicly admit to the legitimacy of Texas independence, in private discussions they expressed a willingness to accept the US annexation of Texas if the boundary would be set at the Nueces River, which had traditionally been the provincial border of Texas. Polk may have been willing to negotiate on the issue of this disputed territory, if Mexico had agreed to sell New Mexico and California. He also planned to use the claims that American citizens had against Mexico as a bargaining concession – the United States would agree to assume the claims as part of an agreement for the sale. Polk had instructed Slidell to insist on the Rio Grande as the boundary, and, shortly after the annexation of Texas became official, he sent American troops into Corpus Christi, just beyond the Nueces River.

The disputed area between the Nueces and the Rio Grande, sometimes called the Nueces Strip, extended from the Gulf Coast to the headwaters of the Rio Grande in what is now Colorado (see Map 5). Slidell also presented an American offer to purchase New Mexico and California, but anti-US feeling in Mexico left Mexican leaders very little latitude on such matters.

Even though he remained in Mexico until the following spring, through a revolution and a change in the Mexican government, Slidell returned to Washington with nothing to show for his efforts.

'HOSTILITIES MAY NOW BE CONSIDERED AS COMMENCED'

In January 1846, Polk received a report from Slidell confirming the refusal of Mexico to discuss any sale of territory. Seeing that his attempts to purchase California and New Mexico had failed, Polk became extremely frustrated. In response, he ordered Taylor to move his troops closer to the Rio Grande, and decided to ask Congress for a declaration of war. He was actually in the process of drafting a war message, using Mexican refusal to pay claims for losses by American citizens as a pretext for the war, when word of an engagement along the border gave him what he considered to be a better justification for going to war. Taylor had moved part of his force to a position on the Rio Grande opposite the Mexican town of Matamoras. The commander of the Mexican troops in the region warned Taylor to remove his forces. Taylor refused, and on 24 April Mexican forces crossed the Rio Grande and attacked the American troops in the disputed territory. In May 1846, Polk received a report of this engagement from Taylor, who wrote that a 'very large force of the enemy' had attacked a party of dragoons patrolling along the Rio Grande. Sixteen men had been killed or wounded, and the survivors had been captured. 'Hostilities,' he wrote, 'may now be considered as commenced' (quoted in Christiansen and Christiansen, 1998: 62). When word of the engagement along the border became public, many in Congress called for war against Mexico. In his message to Congress, Polk requested a declaration that a state of war already existed. He charged that 'American blood has been shed on American soil.' With a supreme disregard for accuracy, he said that war 'not withstanding all our efforts to avoid it, exists by act of Mexico herself.' The House approved a declaration of war with a very sectional vote of 174 to 14. In the Senate, after a day of debate, the declaration passed by 42 to 2. While a heavy majority supported the declaration, the vote was sectional in that all of the opposing votes came from the northeast.

DIVISIONS IN THE US OVER THE WAR

As the vote in Congress indicated, public opinion over the Mexican War was sharply divided. It divided along both party and sectional lines. The Whig party charged that Polk had provoked the war. By compromising on the Oregon question, and going to war on southwest issues, Polk had given many the impression that he was more concerned about expansion of slave territory than about potential free state territory in the north. The Whigs often called the war 'Mr. Polk's War' or 'the Democrat's War.' In December 1847, Abraham Lincoln, as a freshman Whig representative from Illinois, used his first speech in Congress to ask President Polk to indicate exactly where the spot was where 'American blood' had been shed on 'American soil,' implying that the title to that soil was not entirely clear.

Whig opposition to the war declined as time went on. Once war was declared, the Whig Party toned down their dissent, perhaps recalling how opposition to the War of 1812 had destroyed the Federalist Party. Also, two of the leading military commanders, Zachary Taylor and Winfield Scott, were Whigs. Sensing that these two men might become presidential contenders in the future, the Whigs quieted their criticism of the war. However, the war became increasingly unpopular in its later stages, as the number of casualties and the financial costs mounted, and the Whigs began to criticize Polk more openly. In January 1848, the House of Representatives – which had authorized the war with an overwhelming vote a year earlier – narrowly passed a resolution declaring that it had been 'unnecessarily and unconstitutionally begun by the President of the United States' (quoted in McCoy, 1960: 155).

Democrats were faced with a political paradox once the war started. Since a Democratic president had asked for the declaration of war, it was very important that the war be won so that his party not be blamed for failure. But on the other hand, the generals who would have to win the war were Whigs, and victory might well make either one of them a future candidate for the presidency.

Generally, the war was welcomed in the southwest, and strenuously opposed in New England. All of the fourteen votes in the House of Representatives against the declaration of war were from the northeast. Led by John Quincy Adams, the former president who was at this time a member of the House from Massachusetts, the men who voted against the war became known as the 'Fourteen Immortals' in American political lore. Daniel Webster, another important Whig leader in Congress, was ill and therefore absent when the vote was taken on the declaration of war, but upon his return he became a frequent critic of Polk's conduct of the war. In addition to New England's political leaders, its intellectual establishment was also strongly opposed to the war. Ralph Waldo Emerson condemned the war, and Henry David Thoreau went to jail in Concord, Massachusetts, rather than pay taxes that he believed would support a war to extend slavery. Out of this experience, he wrote his famous essay on 'Civil Disobedience,' claiming that one had a duty to oppose laws that were morally unjust.

Sectional and party affiliations did not entirely determine the position of American politicians on the war. John C. Calhoun, a Democratic senator from South Carolina and a staunch advocate of southern interests, argued against the declaration of war in the Senate. Calhoun clearly challenged Polk's charge that the state of war existed by act of Mexico alone, and at one point called the war 'unwise and unjust.' However, he sensed the war would be approved by most of the public and did not wish to endanger his political future by opposing it. He abstained when the vote was taken in the Senate. Similarly, Thomas Hart Benton, a Missouri Democrat in the Senate, raised questions about the wisdom and honor of the war, but eventually voted for the declaration.

CONDUCT OF THE WAR

American military forces achieved rapid victories in many campaigns in the Mexican War. This fact, combined with the general conception of a powerful United States taking advantage of a weaker neighbor, might tempt one to see the outcome of the Mexican War as a foregone conclusion. This interpretation overlooks many factors. The United States was much wealthier than Mexico, and had nearly three times the population (approximately 7,000,000 in Mexico compared to 20,000,000 in the US). However, the United States had a regular army of only 7,300 men, while the Mexican army numbered 32,000.

The distances involved presented American forces with great challenges. Annexation had meant the United States claimed Texas as its own territory, but in reality it was an isolated region hundreds of miles from the nearest centers of population and supplies. Logistics and communications between Washington and Texas would be difficult enough, to say nothing of the eventual need to take an American army deep into Mexican territory. In coastal lowlands, various diseases also threatened American troops. Historian T. R. Fehrenbach notes 'bugs and bad water killed more invaders than Mexican copper balls' (Fehrenbach, 1995: 395).

Within a few weeks of the declaration of war, Taylor had engaged and defeated Mexican armies much larger than his own, while suffering relatively few casualties. Taylor's victories in Texas relieved the immediate threat of a Mexican re-capture of Texas; this gave the US more time to raise and equip the volunteer army needed. Even Polk's Whig opponents in Congress voted for appropriations, while continually raising doubts about the wisdom of the war.

The future political potential of these generals who happened to be Whigs had significant impact on Polk's relationship with his military leaders. Zachary Taylor, in Polk's opinion, had remarkable success in attracting favorable publicity. As the public's view of Taylor rose higher, Polk found more and more to criticize about his ability to command.

Polk's war plans called for three main theaters of war. The first goal was to send an American army into northern Mexico to engage the major body of the Mexican army. Secondly, American forces were to move into New Mexico. The third front was California. Once the United States held these portions of northern Mexico, Polk believed that the Mexican government would be ready to negotiate a peace, and out of these negotiations the United States would gain control of the desired territory.

While there was no strategic plan in place at the beginning of the war, early actions followed these general outlines (see Map 5). Within two days of the declaration of war, Col. Stephen Kearny, commanding a regiment of cavalry at Ft Leavenworth in the Indian Territory, was ordered to undertake a campaign to capture Santa Fé, the capital of New Mexico province. At roughly the same time, US naval commanders in the Gulf of Mexico and in the Pacific received orders to blockade Mexican ports. Shortly after receiving his original orders, Kearny received further instructions. Once New Mexico was in US hands, he was to proceed to California to assist in the conquest of that region.

America was entering the war in a very poor state of readiness, which gave the Mexican forces hope of an easy victory. Polk contemplated raising an army of 23,000 volunteers to serve from six months to one year. Congress authorized the enlistment of up to 50,000 volunteers for one year or the duration of the war, and appropriated $10,000,000 to fund the war. In general the American army fought much better in the Mexican War than it had in the War of 1812. A major factor behind this change was the professionalization of the officer corps and training at the new military academy at West Point, which had been established in 1802. The army officers of this era were often trained, experienced men – not political 'hacks' appointed because of their connections to powerful politicians. Early victories by Taylor's forces in Texas showed the Mexican army that a quick and easy victory was not likely, and also gave the United States more time to raise, equip, and transport the volunteers enlisting for service.

In early May 1846, Taylor led a force of approximately 2,300 men to relieve the troops in the disputed territory which had been besieged since the hostilities had begun. In two decisive battles, at Palo Alto (8 May) and Resaca de la Palma (9 May), Taylor's troops inflicted heavy casualties on the much larger Mexican force. By mid-May, the Mexican forces had abandoned Matamoras and retreated to the south. On 18 May, Taylor's army crossed the Rio Grande into Mexico and occupied Matamoras (see Map 5). Taylor waited there for two months, with disastrous results as disease killed thousands of his troops. Finally, he marched his forces into healthier country in the province of Nuevo León, and attacked the city of Monterrey. This was a strategic location that was the key to the control of northeastern Mexico. After a four-day battle that included intense house-to-house fighting, the American troops captured Monterrey on 24 September 1846.

Having pushed Mexican forces out of Texas and secured much of northern Mexico, Taylor agreed to an armistice for eight weeks. He pledged that US troops would move no further to the south for this period. However, when Polk learned of this, he was greatly displeased. He wanted further quick victories in order to pressure the Mexican government into negotiating. By the time Taylor received word of the administration's disapproval of the armistice, Santa Anna had assumed command of the Mexican troops in northern Mexico. Taylor informed Santa Anna that the truce would be ended on 13 November. Three days after the end of the truce, Taylor's forces attacked and captured Saltillo in the province of Coahuila.

Polk was convinced that a strike into the heart of Mexico was necessary to bring the war to a quick conclusion. He backed General Winfield Scott's plan to attack Vera Cruz. Taylor was ordered to go on the defensive at Monterrey, and to transfer 9,000 of his troops to Scott's command for the Vera Cruz campaign.

In January 1847, Santa Anna's scouts intercepted a message from Scott to Taylor, and learned of the plans to attack Vera Cruz. Facing the choice of moving south to defend Vera Cruz, or north to attack Taylor's forces – now cut to less than half their former number by the dispatch of the troops to join Scott – Santa Anna decided to attack Taylor. He massed 20,000 troops at San Luis Potosi and maneuvered to bring Taylor to battle. In late February 1847, Taylor's force of about 4,800 men entrenched in defensive positions near the village of Buena Vista to meet Santa Anna's attack.

Santa Anna moved north with more than 15,000 men to attack Taylor. Arriving at Buena Vista, he sent Taylor a demand for an unconditional surrender. Taylor refused and Santa Anna attacked. After two days of heavy fighting on 22–3 February, Santa Anna was forced to retreat, having lost approximately 1,600 men killed or wounded. In holding off a force more than twice its own size, Taylor's command had lost only 272 men killed and 387 wounded. The Battle of Buena Vista marked the end of significant fighting in northeastern Mexico (see Map 5). It was also the last major engagement in which Taylor commanded his troops. He remained in northern Mexico for nine more months, but became increasingly convinced that Polk's administration sought to undercut his ability to command effectively. Finally he asked to be relieved of his command, and left Mexico in November 1847. He returned to the United States to receive a hero's welcome from the public.

By early 1847, most of Polk's initial objectives had been gained. United States forces were firmly in control of the disputed border regions as well as much of northern Mexico. Further to the West, efforts to detach New Mexico and California from Mexican control were also meeting with success.

Stephen Kearny's 'Army of the West' took a month to march from Ft Leavenworth on the Missouri River in the Indian Territory, to Bent's Fort on the Arkansas River in what is now southeastern Colorado. Bent's Fort was an important trading post on the Santa Fé trail. Upon his arrival there at the end of July 1846, Kearny issued a proclamation to the people of New Mexico. He stated that he was coming into their province 'for the purpose of seeking union with and ameliorating the conditions of its inhabitants' (quoted in Morris and Morris, 1996: 224). He also sent a letter to the Mexican provincial governor promising protection to all who cooperated.

In early August, Kearny's army marched south into New Mexico. By the middle of the month, he had reached Las Vegas (in New Mexico, not to be confused with the modern-day city of Las Vegas in Nevada). There Kearny proclaimed that New Mexico was now part of the United States. Historians have often written that New Mexico came into US possession without a shot being fired. It is true that several thousand Mexican troops at Apache Canyon, southwest of Santa Fé, dispersed without offering resistance to Kearny. However, in the winter of 1846–7, Mexican settlers in the province rose up against American rule. This rebellion was put down by troops under Col. Sterling Price in February 1847, and was the last organized resistance to American occupation of New Mexico.

Kearny's forces occupied the provincial capital at Santa Fé on 18 August 1846. He set up a temporary territorial government under Charles Bent, one of the proprietors of Bent's Fort who had been living in Taos. Having secured New Mexico, Kearny went on toward California, according to his original orders. In early October, he met Kit Carson, who was on his way to Washington with a message from Frémont announcing the occupation of California. Believing his force was not all needed in California, Kearny sent 200 of his men back and proceeded west with the remaining 100.

There had not been a significant number of American settlers in the Mexican province of Alta California until the late 1830s. The first significant settlement of Americans was in the San Joaquin Valley, beginning in 1843. At the time the Mexican War broke out there were about 500 Americans living in Alta California, along with 8,000 to 12,000 Mexicans and perhaps 24,000 Indians.

Mexico had never had firm control of this distant province. Residents of the province, both Mexican citizens and foreigners, often resented the laws imposed upon them by the distant central government. There had been attempted revolts in 1836 and 1845.

Captain John C. Frémont set out in 1845 on an expedition to map the valleys of the Red River and Arkansas River. However, he also pushed on to the west, explored the area around the Great Salt Lake, and then went into

California. He reached Monterey in California in January 1846. Within a short time, however, he was ordered to leave the province by the Mexican military commander. Frémont left and proceeded toward Oregon, but on the way he met a messenger with dispatches from President Polk. He later claimed to have eaten the message, in order to maintain secrecy, so it is not known precisely what it was he was ordered to do. But Frémont went back to California to try to instigate a revolt against the Mexican authorities.

There had been tensions for years between the Mexican provincial officials and the military leaders in California, and these had been exacerbated by news of a revolution in Mexico the preceding December. By the time Frémont got back to California, a revolt had already begun. Some Mexican political leaders had called for a convention to move toward creating an independent state in California, and fighting had broken out between supporters of this movement and the military forces. At the same time, American settlers had proclaimed the independence of their settlements and proclaimed the creation of the Republic of California. Because of the depiction of a bear on their flag, this uprising became known as the Bear Flag Revolt; when Frémont arrived in Sonoma in late June, he aligned himself with it. In early July, he was chosen as the leader of the Republic of California.

In May 1846, Commodore John D. Sloat, commander of the US naval forces along the Pacific Coast, heard of the opening of hostilities between the US and Mexico. He took no immediate action because he had been instructed to avoid the appearance of aggression. The next month, when he learned that US naval vessels were blockading the port of Vera Cruz on Mexico's eastern coast, Sloat sailed to Monterey in California. On 7 July he sent a force ashore that took control of Monterey and proclaimed California to be part of the United States.

In the fall of 1846, the Mexican forces almost succeeded in driving Americans out of California. However, Kearny's troops, combined with naval forces of Commodore Robert Stockton, succeeded in pushing out the Mexican defenders by January 1847. Resistance in California was virtually over from that point.

While the American forces were victorious on every front, the war was far from over. The Mexican army lacked solid leadership and good equipment, but the Mexican soldiers made up for a lot of these deficiencies with determination and a fervent national pride. Scott's attack on Vera Cruz, and his plans to drive into the heart of Mexico, were intended to break the will of the Mexicans to continue to resist (see Map 5).

While headquartered at Tampico on the Mexican coast and making plans for the attack on Vera Cruz, Scott issued General Order Number 20 to his forces. The order was intended to secure the cooperation of the Mexican people, and to outline punishment for American soldiers guilty of mistreatment of Mexican nationals. This was significant because the American army, which before the Mexican War had never fought outside of the boundaries of the United States except for limited engagements during the War of 1812, was for the first time setting up regulations for the occupation of enemy territory.

In early March 1847, Scott landed his forces at Vera Cruz and began the siege of the city. By the middle of that month, he had Vera Cruz largely surrounded and cut off from reinforcements or re-supply. The Mexican troops in the city surrendered on 29 March. Scott then moved inland from Vera Cruz, fighting a series of important battles as he moved the approximately 150 miles from the coast to Mexico City. In early April, Scott faced Santa Anna near Cerro Gordo. The American forces numbered about 9,000, while Santa Anna had 13,000 in his command. In one of the interesting ironies of the war, two US military engineers made an important reconnaissance of the potential battlefield. These two engineers – Captain Robert E. Lee and Captain George McClellan – would later face each other along the Potomac River as commanders of major armies in the American Civil War. After heavy fighting at Cerro Gordo, Santa Anna's troops were routed, with over 3,000 men (including over 200 officers) being captured by the Americans.

Several important engagements followed throughout the summer of 1847 as Scott continued to move inland. The last major engagement before the capture of Mexico City was the Battle of Chapultepec, on the outskirts of the Mexican capital. Scott's troops attacked this fortified hill on the morning of 12 September. About 1,000 Mexican troops defended the summit. After scaling the hill with ladders and pick axes, the American troops took the hill. About 100 cadets from the Mexican Military Academy, which sat on the crest of the hill, fought bravely in the defense of Chapultepec, and become known as 'Los Niños' in Mexican lore.

Scott's forces moved on immediately to attack the Mexican capital. The walls surrounding the city were breached, and the American forces took control of the national palace on 14 September. Although the Mexican people were clearly not pacified, serious resistance to American occupation was soon over. Santa Anna fled the city. In early October, he renounced his position as president and fled the country.

PEACE NEGOTIATIONS

In April 1847, President Polk had sent Nicholas P. Trist to Mexico to attempt to negotiate a peace with the Mexican government. Trist was well qualified for the post, having served as American consul in Havana, Cuba. However, over the course of the summer and early fall of 1847, Polk became dissatisfied with Trist's mission, and fearful that his mission might encourage the Mexican government to believe that the US wanted peace on easy terms. Thus, in early October, Polk sent Trist an order recalling him from his mission.

Trist accepted his recall without enmity, and hoped that his going back to Washington might be fruitful in that he could provide the Polk administration with first-hand accounts of the situation in Mexico. However, events began to move more quickly than he envisioned. In late November, the leader of the interim Mexican government informed Trist that peace commissioners had been appointed, and that Mexico was 'in principle' ready to discuss peace. The head of the British legation in Mexico City promised to offer his 'good offices' to help broker a peace. Additionally, General Winfield Scott supported Trist and believed that his recall had been a mistake. In response to these matters, Trist decided to ignore his recall. He continued his negotiations, and by the end of January the basic outlines of a treaty were in place. Trist and the Mexican commissioners signed the Treaty of Guadalupe Hidalgo on 2 February 1848. By the terms of this treaty, the United States gained what became the states of California, New Mexico, Nevada, and Arizona. Mexico also agreed to recognize the Rio Grande as the southern border of Texas. In return, the United States agreed to assume damages that Texas residents had against the Mexican government for losses; these claims amounted to approximately $3,000,000. The United States also paid Mexico $15,000,000 for the land annexed, in what is often cited as an example of paying 'conscience money.'

When Polk received the treaty, he was infuriated with Trist for presuming to negotiate the treaty after having been officially recalled. However, political considerations forced him to put his personal feelings aside. The war had become increasingly unpopular as casualty figures and costs mounted. Polk knew the American public had no desire to see a lengthy occupation of Mexico, so he submitted the treaty to the Senate for its ratification. With a few modifications, the Senate ratified the treaty on 10 March 1848. The Mexican Senate approved the modified treaty in late May, and on 12 June 1848, the American army ended its occupation of Mexico City – almost exactly nine months since Scott had taken control of it.

CONSEQUENCES OF THE WAR

American casualties were relatively light in the Mexican War. About 1,700 men had died as a result of wounds suffered in battle. While the number was relatively low, in terms of deaths as a percentage of the total number of soldiers involved, the casualties were very high. Furthermore, over 11,000 men had died of disease.

Historian David Pletcher has noted, 'Victory in the Mexican War did not launch the United States as a Great Power – this would require another half-century of growth – but it certainly helped to promote the nation from a third-rate to a second-rate power that would have to be reckoned with in its own neighborhood' (Pletcher, 1973: 5).

With the completion of the Mexican War and the later Gadsden Purchase, the United States had expanded across the continent in the southwest, just as settlement of the Oregon question had extended US territory to the Pacific in the northwest. The war had cost almost 13,000 American lives, and approximately 50,000 Mexican lives; it had cost America about $100,000,000. The war also created an enmity between the United States and much of Latin America that lingers even today.

The successful conclusion of the Mexican War brought vast new territories to the United States. Acquisition of Texas, Oregon, and the region ceded by Mexico in the Treaty of Guadalupe Hidalgo made the United States truly a continental nation. Roughly a million square miles of territory had been taken from Mexico – an area larger than the Louisiana Purchase. The unorganized territory west of the Mississippi constituted nearly one half of the total lands of the nation. Organization for the administration of these territories would be a slow and complex task (Arizona and New Mexico, for example, would not become states until well into the twentieth century). More seriously, however, the acquisition of these new lands rekindled the fires of sectional controversy, as Congress debated the extension of slavery into the territories. Each time the nation expanded, it again faced this thorny question: should the new territory be slave or free?

Expansion of slavery into territory gained from Mexico was very important to the south. For many years, the growth of population in the north had meant that the south would never have parity in the House of Representatives, where representation is based on population. Thus, the south was very concerned to maintain a balance of free and slave territory, so that it could have power in the Senate roughly equal to that of the north.

On both moral and political grounds, the southerners feared acquiescing to the exclusion of slavery from any of the new territories. To do so, they believed, was tantamount to admitting the injustice of slavery. Even before the war was over, question of expansion of slavery into the southwest had returned to haunt Congress.

In August 1846, David Wilmot, a Democratic member of the House from northeastern Pennsylvania, introduced an amendment to an appropriation bill. The amendment, which became known as the Wilmot Proviso, provided that no land gained through the war with Mexico would be open for slavery. In several sessions of Congress from 1846 on, the Wilmot Proviso was introduced, with some modifications. It passed the House on two occasions, but never passed the Senate. While it never became law, the Wilmot Proviso was significant in that it kept debate stirred up on the issue of the extension of slavery into any new territories the US might gain from the war.

The first sectional battle involving the territory taken from Mexico involved the new territory in California. More than 80,000 Americans had flooded into California as a result of the 1848 Gold Rush. With this rapid influx of settlers, California quickly surpassed the minimum population needed to apply for statehood. Californians drafted a constitution and petitioned Congress for admission to the Union as a free state. The south generally opposed this; southerners wanted California to be a slave state, or failing this, they wanted the Missouri Compromise line extended through California.

In Congress, Henry Clay and Stephen Douglas attempted to work out a compromise that would avoid conflict over California, and also deal with some other aspects of the sectional controversy. The agreement that finally emerged and became known as the 'Compromise of 1850' admitted California as a free state. In the remainder of the Mexican Cession, the principle of 'popular sovereignty' would apply – meaning that the settlers who actually went to these territories could determine whether they were to be slave or free states. Another part of the compromise dealt with defining the border between Texas and the New Mexico Territory (see Map 6). Other terms were added in order to placate interests in the south and the north. Antislavery people in the north were incensed at the buying and selling of slaves in the District of Columbia, where slave sales were often conducted on the steps of the US capitol building. To make the compromise more palatable to these northerners, it would no longer be legal to bring slaves into the District of Columbia for the purpose of selling them. To make the compromise more acceptable to southern interests, a new Fugitive Slave Law was added, which would have tougher penalties for those convicted of aiding the escape of slaves, and added measures for enforcement of the law.

There was a great deal of celebration after passage of the several pieces of legislation that together made up the Compromise of 1850. However, there really was less cause for rejoicing than many thought. The Compromise did not really solve several of the problems addressed, but merely postponed them. For example, while the concept of 'popular sovereignty' seemed simple enough, there was still debate over precisely what it meant. When could a territory outlaw slavery – could a territorial legislature do it, or must it be done in the constitution that the prospective state sends to Congress for its approval?

THE GADSDEN PURCHASE

The acquisition of the Mexican Cession was the last major territorial expansion in the contiguous United States (that is, the US exclusive of Alaska and Hawaii). However, in 1853, additional territory was purchased from Mexico in what has become known as the Gadsden Purchase. Since the 1840s, there had been discussions about a possible transcontinental railway, although the first one would not be completed until 1869. Before the Civil War, sectional debates complicated the matter of the route for the first transcontinental railroad. Southerners were convinced that the best route would be west from Texas through the valley of the Gila River in present-day Arizona. President Franklin Pierce named James Gadsden, a railroad executive, to negotiate with Mexico for the sale of this territory. Santa Anna was back in power in Mexico, and agreed to the sale of a strip of approximately 29,000 square miles. Besides the location of a possible railroad route, the Gadsden Purchase Treaty also settled some matters concerning the border between the United States and Mexico. A map referred to in the Treaty of Guadalupe Hidalgo that was to be used for fixing the border west of where the Rio Grande River turns to the north near El Paso was incorrect. In the Gadsden Purchase, the United States paid $10,000,000 for the land along the Gila River and the Mesilla Valley. Although the first transcontinental railway would be built on a more central route, in 1883 the Southern Pacific Railroad was built through the area of Gadsden Purchase.

The Mexican War and its aftermath brought vast new territories into the domain of the United States. After the Gadsden Purchase, the continental expansion of the United States was over, with the single exception of the purchase of Alaska from Russia in 1867. The expansionist fervor that a few years earlier had called for war with both Great Britain and Mexico over Oregon and Texas disappeared almost as quickly as it had arisen. Perhaps one reason for this decline in expansionist rhetoric was the realization that the new territories taken from Mexico were a mixed blessing. With these new additions came a renewal of the sectional disputes over the expansion of areas open to slavery. The Compromise of 1850, which was supposed to settle those disputes, actually only delayed the final reckoning. The disruptiveness of this latest territorial acquisition, in addition to the monetary cost, the high number of lives lost, and the enmity that the war engendered between the United States and much of Latin America, may well have given pause to the advocates of expansionism.

Even at the time, there seemed to be some recognition in America that the outcome of the war was not entirely an occasion for great rejoicing. It seemed hard for many Americans to deny the fact that, despite all the rhetorical justifications, the United States had gone to war with a poor, weak neighbor (and sister republic) for the purpose of acquiring territory. Historian Sam W. Haynes has noted that the war, and the 'spirit of aggressive expansionism that led to it,' exposed an aspect of American character that seemed inconsistent with the ideals that Americans had long espoused. The war, Haynes wrote, 'transformed the United States into a continental empire, but at the cost of its claims of moral stewardship' (quoted in Christiansen and Christiansen, 1998: 232). Many Americans were proud that US territory now stretched from sea to sea. But there was an uneasy awareness, for some at least, that the question of how that territory had been acquired was not one that could be answered with unalloyed patriotic pride.

CHAPTER SIX

CONCLUSION

In the period between the end of the American Revolution and the outbreak of the Civil War, the United States underwent dramatic changes. The major focus of this book has been the territorial expansion that made the United States a continental nation and a world power by 1860. While this expansion was occurring, however, other remarkable changes were also taking place. The population of the United States increased nearly eight times over in this era, from slightly fewer than four million at the time of the first federal census in 1790 to over 31 million in 1860. Even as agriculture and other forms of development transformed newly opened lands to the west, urbanization and industrialization were proceeding apace in the east.

In many ways, Americans seemed to expect and even to embrace these changes. While few pretended to be able to discern precisely what changes would occur, there seemed to be a common recognition and acceptance of the fact that changes would come. From the beginning of colonization in the Americas, there was a sense that this was a new beginning, that things in this new hemisphere could evolve and develop in new ways, unencumbered by precedent and tradition.

As has been shown in earlier chapters, the United States has always been an expansionist nation. However, the decade of the 1840s proved to be the high tide of American continental expansionism. The annexation of Texas, the settlement of the Oregon issue, and the conquest of the northern provinces of the Republic of Mexico added huge new western territories to the United States' national domain. The controversies engendered by this rapid expansion meant that it would be some time before the nation fully 'digested' this rich repast. But once this chapter in American territorial growth ended, expansionism seemed gradually to fade away as a significant force in American politics and public rhetoric.

WHY DID EXPANSIONIST FERVOR DECLINE?

It may seem strange that the expansionist fervor, which had been so strong in the 1840s, could die out relatively quickly in the 1850s. No doubt a major factor is the growth of the sectional crisis and the fears of a possible civil war to come, which naturally diverted the attention of many Americans. But there also seemed to be a general consensus that American expansion had reached its natural limits. Expansionists had advanced the concept of 'continentalism' as a reason for the extension of US territory to the Pacific Coast. However, once that was accomplished, that same concept could be used to suggest that enough was enough. Perhaps historian Richard White's explanation is the best – that the very success of the expansionists did them in (White, 1991: 83). After a decade in which the expansionists had succeeded to an extent few would have dreamed possible, there no longer seemed much reason for further territorial growth.

AMERICAN EXPANSIONISM: A CASE OF MANIFEST DESTINY?

Looking back on the dramatic expansion of the United States from 1783 to 1861, it is easy to fall prey to the conclusion that this was inevitable. Expansion across the continent, between the 49th parallel and the Rio Grande River, seemed to have a natural logic to it. But was it destined? Was the growth of the United States across the North American continent really something that proceeded like an unstoppable juggernaut across the early decades of the nation's existence? Or was it a matter of deliberate political and military policy and endeavor?

In the introduction to this volume, the following questions were posed: Were all Americans in favor of expansionism? How does the concept of a 'Manifest Destiny' of the United States to expand as a unified nation relate to the growth of sectionalism in this same era? If Americans truly saw expansion as something that was evident or manifest, why was there significant opposition to virtually every expansionary move in this era?

In the 1840s, expansionists had coined the term 'Manifest Destiny' to encourage people to believe that it was manifest or evident that the United States was destined to expand 'from sea to shining sea.' Historians have often fallen under the hypnotic spell of these powerful words, and many scholars have portrayed America's expansion in terms of destiny and fate. While this mythic interpretation of American expansion remains widely popular, the facts simply do not support it. While it is clear that many Americans at times believed in something like the concept of 'Manifest Destiny' – even if they had never heard or read that precise phrase – it is equally clear that not all Americans shared this belief. As has been noted throughout this book, every instance of territorial expansion was opposed by some segment of the American public. Obviously, the opposition was much stronger in some cases than in others. For example, the opposition of the Federalists to the Louisiana Purchase, which was largely just party politics in action, must be contrasted to the heated sectional debates over Texas and Mexico, which involved moralistic arguments and deeply held principles on both sides.

Historians Robert V. Hine and John Mack Faragher have noted, ' "Manifest Destiny" was not, as historians so often imply, a deeply held American folk belief. Rather, it was the self-conscious creation of political propagandists like O'Sullivan, determined to uncouple the politics of expansion from the growing sectional controversy over slavery' (Hine and Faragher, 2000: 200). Robert Johannsen's characterization of O'Sullivan's coining of the term 'Manifest Destiny' is apt: 'He [O'Sullivan] had provided a catchphrase for a concept that was as old as the nation itself, even older' (Johannsen, 1997: 9).

In one of the most important studies of the concept of Manifest Destiny, historian Frederick Merk argued that 'continentalist' and 'imperialist' expansion did not really embody the 'national spirit' of the United States. Rather, he believed that Manifest Destiny was a 'trap' that temporarily took the nation away from its true national spirit – the sense of mission (Merk, 1963: 261). Historians still debate Merk's contention of the supremacy of the idea of Mission, but he did raise some important issues about the weight of the support for Manifest Destiny. Votes for candidates that supported expansion, for example, do not necessarily translate into public support for that issue – because people choose a candidate based on a variety of issues. Political speeches and newspaper editorials might be read as indicators of the public mood, but Merk warns us that they might just as well be attempts to shape and direct public sentiment. Perhaps it is best to see the extent of the support for Manifest Destiny as Richard White suggests – that the expansionists were a powerful group, but the majority they forged in the 1840s was only a temporary one (White, 1991: 83).

Opposition to expansion was based on a variety of issues, over the course of time from the end of the American Revolution to the 1850s. Sometimes it was simply party politics; at other times, the details or mechanics of a particular expansionist proposal might have been debated. But by far the strongest source of opposition grew out of the sectional crisis. The debate over the admission of Missouri to the Union sparked the first great debate over the expansion of slave territory. The Missouri Compromise of 1820 settled this particular episode of the debate, but it was clear that the issue would re-emerge whenever any new territory was added. After the settlement of the Oregon boundary issue, it appeared that any further territory added to the United States would come from the southern part of the continent. Those in the south came to believe that slavery could continue to exist only if new territory was added and slavery was allowed to expand into these regions. At the same time, many in the north came to the same basic conclusion – expansion of US territory would mean the expansion of slave territory. But the northern application of this conclusion was different – rather than see new slave territory added, expansionism should be disavowed. Since the sectional issue threatened to kill the Union, the Union would have to be preserved by killing expansionism (Graebner, 1955: 187). Historian David Potter noted the paradox to which this brought the nation by 1860:

> By the time the southern states seceded, Manifest Destiny had reached a supreme paradox: northern unionists who believed in American nationalism resisted most proposals for further territorial growth of the nation, while states' rights southerners who denied that the Union was a nation sought to extend the national domain from pole to pole. The expansionists were not nationalists, and the nationalists were not expansionists.   (Potter, 1976: 197)

Thus, even though the United States had grown dramatically in the early nineteenth century, by mid-century there was a growing debate about the very nature of 'nationhood.' Northern leaders saw the United States as a single whole with a sovereign federal government. Southern politicians and opinion makers, on the other hand, saw the Union as a league of states, each of which retained their own sovereignty – including the right to secede. Sectional disputes ultimately derailed expansionism, and threatened the very existence of the nation itself. No common understanding or national consensus could be found on how to deal with the issues of slavery in the territories. As Richard White concludes, 'The march toward an "empire of liberty" faltered before increasingly volatile sectional divisions. The imperial republic proved unable to forge a consensus for nationalist expansion' (White, 1991: 73).

America's territorial expansion was no more destined than was its political development, the growth of its military power, or its dramatic economic progress. Continental expansion, like all of these other developments, was the result of direct, sustained action by a series of American politicians, statesmen, opinion makers, entrepreneurs, and pioneers over the course of nearly two generations. At times, the troubles of other nations provided unique opportunities ('out of European distress came American success'), but such windfalls were not the driving force behind American expansion. Leaders such as Thomas Jefferson and James K. Polk – who surpass all other American presidents as expansionists – set specific goals that they believed were obtainable by diplomacy or military force. As Hine and Faragher have noted, attributing America's territorial growth to something like Manifest Destiny ignores 'the purposeful federal policy and the ruthless power that were necessary prerequisites to the conquest of the continent. The United States did not acquire an empire by doing what came naturally' (Hine and Farragher, 2000: 200).

Expansionists were able to put together the political coalitions needed to back acquisition of new territories because they sought specific goals and made convincing arguments that achieving these goals was necessary. The Jeffersonian presidents – Jefferson himself, Madison, and Monroe – believed that an abundance of land was necessary to preserve the type of agrarian republic that Jefferson had envisioned. The Jacksonians – Jackson himself, Van Buren, and Polk – also believed that plentiful new lands were necessary for the expansion of opportunity for the common man. American political leaders additionally held that continental expansion was necessary for American security. Historian Thomas Hietala has persuasively argued that anxiety, rather than a booming confidence, was an important motivation behind American expansionism (Hietala, 1985: 262–4). Removing potential European enemies from the borders of the United States, rounding out reasonable and defensible boundaries, and providing for orderly political and economic development in the new territories – these were all real concerns of the expansionists.

WAS EARLY AMERICAN EXPANSIONISM IMPERIALISTIC?

In the late nineteenth century, the United States began for the first time to acquire territory outside the continental limits of North America. This included 'possessions' such as the Midway Islands and Hawaii, and 'protectorates' such as Cuba, Puerto Rico, and the Philippine Islands, which came under US control as a result of the Spanish–American War in 1898.

Historians have often argued that the United States did not become an 'imperialistic' power until these later acquisitions of an island empire. This argument is based on the fact that earlier continental expansion involved lands that would eventually become states of the Union, equal in all respects to earlier states, and the people in these lands would eventually become citizens of the United States. They would not be held indefinitely in some sort of colonial status. This changed when America took control of areas that were never seriously considered as candidates for statehood.

There is some merit in this distinction simply because early American expansion was aimed at land and resources, not acquisition of a subject class of colonials. As several scholars have noted, the United States would have been just as happy if the Indians, the Creoles of Louisiana, or the Mexicans living in the Mexican Cession lands, were simply not there at all.

That being said, it is not accurate to say that earlier American expansion was not imperialistic. In 1965, diplomatic historian Samuel Flagg Bemis wrote that 'American expansion over a practically empty continent despoiled no nation unjustly' (cited in Hietala, 1985: 259). Today, most scholars would recognize such a statement simply as patriotic hyperbole. Perhaps compared to crowded Europe, the American continent had seemed 'practically empty,' but the point is – it was *not* empty, and the peoples who were deemed 'in the way' were treated in an imperialistic fashion.

It has not been easy for Americans to deal with the legacy of the expansionist fervor that gripped the United States in the early decades of the nineteenth century. Just as earlier generations wrestled with the very real political and sectional disputes occasioned by each episode of expansionism, thoughtful Americans today continue to be troubled by the questions of injustice and imperialism concerning the means by which this dramatic growth was accomplished. While Americans have often been reluctant to face up to some of the more sordid details about the nature of American expansionism, recent scholarship is making it possible to see a clearer picture of how American expansionism proceeded. Truly, a part of that story is the hard work and determination of pioneer settlers, the bravery of soldiers, and the leadership of visionary statesmen. But we cannot ignore that another part of that story is injustice toward people believed to be blocking the road to American greatness. Although we may be uncomfortable with the resulting picture, true understanding can result only when we take pains to perceive the story in all its fullness.

DOCUMENTS

JOHN WINTHROP, 'A MODELL OF CHRISTIAN CHARITY,' 1630

The concept of 'manifest destiny' includes, and perhaps stems in part from, the belief that America had a special purpose or mission in the world. One of the earliest examples of that concept can be found in the Puritan leader John Winthrop's 1630 sermon, given on board ship before the colonizers of the Massachusetts Bay Colony reached the New World.

Now the onely way to avoyde this shipwracke and to provide for our posterity is to followe the counsel of Micah, to doe Justly, to love mercy, to walke humbly with our God. For this end, wee must be knit together in this worke as one man, we must entertaine each other in brotherly Affeccion, wee must be willing to abridge ourselves of our superfluities, for the supply of others necessities, wee must uphold a familiar Commerce together in all meeknes, gentlenes, patience and liberality, wee must delight in each other, make others Condicions our owne, rejoice together, mourne together, labour and suffer together, allwayes haveing before our eyes our Commission and Community in the worke, our Community as members of the same body, soe shall wee keepe the unitie of the spirit in the bond of peace, the Lord will be our God and delight to dwell among us as his owne people and will commaund a blessing upon us in all our wayes, soe that wee shall see much more of his wisdome, power, goodnes and truthe than formerly wee have been acquainted with. Wee shall finde that the God of Israel is among us, when tenn of us shall be able to resist a thousand of our enemies, when he shall make us a prayse and glory, that men shall say of succeeding plantacions: the Lord make it like that of New England; for we must Consider that wee shall be as a Citty upon a Hill, the eies of all people are upon us, so that if we deal falsely with our god in this worke wee have undertaken and so cause him to withdrawe his present help from us, wee shall shame the faces of many of gods worthy servants, and cause theire prayers to be turned into Curses upon us till we be consumed out of the good land whither wee are goeing ...

Conrad Cherry (ed.), *God's New Israel: Religious Interpretations of American Destiny*, revised and updated edn (Chapel Hill, NC: University of North Carolina Press, 1998) p. 40.

DOCUMENT 2 **THE NORTHWEST ORDINANCES, 1787**

How to organize the new territories that were added to the United States was an important question facing the early American statesmen. The Northwest Ordinances of 1787 were significant in laying out how the territories north and west of the Ohio River would be organized as territories and eventually incorporated as states, equal to the original 13 states.

Be it ordained by the United States in Congress assembled, That the said territory, for the purposes of temporary government, be one district, subject, however, to be divided into two districts, as future circumstances may, in the opinion of Congress, make it expedient.

... So soon as there shall be five thousand free male inhabitants of full age in the district, upon giving proof thereof to the governor, they shall receive authority, with time and place, to elect a representative from their counties or townships to represent them in the general assembly ...

... And, for extending the fundamental principles of civil and religious liberty, which form the basis whereon these republics, their laws and constitutions are erected; to fix and establish those principles as the basis of all laws, constitutions, and governments, which forever hereafter shall be formed in the said territory: to provide also for the establishment of States, and permanent government therein, and for their admission to a share in the federal councils on an equal footing with the original States, at as early periods as may be consistent with the general interest: It is hereby ordained and declared by the authority aforesaid, That the following articles shall be considered as articles of compact between the original States and the people and States in the said territory and forever remain unalterable, unless by common consent, to wit:

... Art. 2.

The inhabitants of the said territory shall always be entitled to the benefits of the writ of habeas corpus, and of the trial by jury; of a proportionate representation of the people in the legislature; and of judicial proceedings according to the course of the common law.

... Art. 5.

There shall be formed in the said territory, not less than three nor more than five States ...

And, whenever any of the said States shall have sixty thousand free inhabitants therein, such State shall be admitted, by its delegates, into the Congress of the United States, on an equal footing with the original States in all respects whatever, and shall be at liberty to form a permanent constitution and State government: Provided, the constitution and government so to be formed, shall be republican, and in conformity to the principles contained in these articles; and, so far as it can be consistent with the general interest of the confederacy, such admission shall be allowed at an earlier period, and when there may be a less number of free inhabitants in the State than sixty thousand.

Art. 6.

There shall be neither slavery nor involuntary servitude in the said territory, otherwise than in the punishment of crimes whereof the party shall have been duly convicted: Provided, always, That any person escaping into the same, from whom labor or service is lawfully claimed in any one of the original States, such fugitive may be lawfully reclaimed and conveyed to the person claiming his or her labor or service as aforesaid.

Annals of America, vol. 3, *Organizing the New Nation, 1784–1796* (Chicago: Encyclopaedia Britannica, 1969), pp. 191–6.

DOCUMENT 3   JAMES MADISON ON THE VIRTUES OF A LARGE REPUBLIC: *THE FEDERALIST* NUMBER 10, 1787

Many political theorists had argued that republics are a suitable form of government only for small and relatively impoverished nations. In The Federalist *no. 10, James Madison, one of the key figures in the creation of the constitution, argues that in a large republic, the number of contending interest groups can help to control the effect of faction.*

To the People of the State of New York:

AMONG the numerous advantages promised by a well-constructed Union, none deserves to be more accurately developed than its tendency to break and control the violence of faction. The friend of popular governments never finds himself so much alarmed for their character and fate, as when he contemplates their propensity to this dangerous vice. ...

From this view of the subject it may be concluded that a pure democracy, by which I mean a society consisting of a small number of citizens, who assemble and administer the government in person, can admit of no cure for the mischiefs of faction. ...

A republic, by which I mean a government in which the scheme of representation takes place, opens a different prospect, and promises the cure for which we are seeking. Let us examine the points in which it varies from pure democracy, and we shall comprehend both the nature of the cure and the efficacy which it must derive from the Union.

The two great points of difference between a democracy and a republic are: first, the delegation of the government, in the latter, to a small number of citizens elected by the rest; secondly, the greater number of citizens, and greater sphere of country, over which the latter may be extended.

Men of factious tempers, of local prejudices, or of sinister designs, may, by intrigue, by corruption, or by other means, first obtain the suffrages, and then betray the interests, of the people. The question resulting is, whether small or extensive republics are more favorable to the election of proper guardians of the public weal; and it is clearly decided in favor of the latter by two obvious considerations:

In the first place, it is to be remarked that, however small the republic may be, the representatives must be raised to a certain number, in order to guard against the cabals of a few; and that, however large it may be, they must be limited to a certain number, in order to guard against the confusion of a multitude. Hence, the number of representatives in the two cases not being in proportion to that of the two constituents, and being proportionally greater in the small republic, it follows that, if the proportion of fit characters be not less in the large than in the small republic, the former will present a greater option, and consequently a greater probability of a fit choice.

In the next place, as each representative will be chosen by a greater number of citizens in the large than in the small republic, it will be more difficult for unworthy candidates to practice with success the vicious arts by which elections are too often carried; and the suffrages of the people being more free, will be more likely to centre in men who possess the most attractive merit and the most diffusive and established characters. ...

The other point of difference is, the greater number of citizens and extent of territory which may be brought within the compass of republican than of democratic government; and it is this circumstance principally which renders factious combinations less to be dreaded in the former than in the latter. The smaller the society, the fewer probably will be the distinct parties and interests composing it; the fewer the distinct parties and interests, the more frequently will a majority be found of the same party; and the smaller the number of individuals composing a majority, and the smaller the compass within which they are placed, the more easily will they concert and execute their plans of oppression. Extend the sphere, and you take in a greater variety of parties and interests; you make it less probable that a majority of the whole will have a common motive to invade the rights of other citizens; or if such a common motive exists, it will be more difficult for all who feel it to discover their own strength, and to act in unison with each other. ...

Hence, it clearly appears, that the same advantage which a republic has over a democracy, in controlling the effects of faction, is enjoyed by a large over a small republic, – is enjoyed by the Union over the States composing it. Does the advantage consist in the substitution of representatives whose enlightened views and virtuous sentiments render them superior to local prejudices and schemes of injustice? It will not be denied that the representation of the Union will be most likely to possess these requisite endowments. Does it consist in the greater security afforded by a greater variety of parties, against the event of any one party being able to outnumber and oppress the rest? In an equal degree does the increased variety of parties comprised within the Union, increase this security. Does it, in fine, consist in the greater obstacles opposed to the concert and accomplishment of the secret wishes of an unjust and interested majority? Here, again, the extent of the Union gives it the most palpable advantage. ...

Alexander Hamilton, James Madison, and John Jay, *The Federalist Papers*, in *Great Books of the Western World*, vol. 43, *American State Papers* (Chicago: Encyclopaedia Britannica, 1952), pp. 49–53.

DOCUMENT 4 THOMAS JEFFERSON ON THE FRENCH THREAT IN NEW ORLEANS, 1802

The news that Spain had ceded Louisiana to France caused much consternation in the United States. President Thomas Jefferson wrote to his ambassador in France to express his concerns about the matter.

April 8, 1802

The cession of Louisiana, and the Floridas, by Spain to France, works most sorely on the United States. On this subject the Secretary of State has written to you fully, yet I cannot forbear recurring to it personally, so deep is the impression it makes upon my mind. It completely reverses all the political relations of the United States, and will form a new epoch in our political course. Of all nations of any consideration, France is the one which, hitherto, has offered the fewest points on which we could have any conflict of right, and the most points of a communion of interests. From these causes, we have ever looked to her as our *natural friend*, as one with which we could never have an occasion of difference. Her growth, therefore, we viewed as our own, her misfortunes ours. There is on the globe one single spot, the possessor of which is our natural and habitual enemy. It is New Orleans, through which the produce of three-eighths of our territory must pass to market, and from its fertility, it will ere long yield more than half of our whole produce, and contain more than half our inhabitants. France, placing herself in that door, assumes to us the attitude of defiance. Spain might have retained it quietly for years. Her pacific dispositions, her feeble state, would induce her to increase our facilities there, so that her possession of the place would be hardly felt by us, and it would not, perhaps, be very long before some circumstance might arise, which might make the cession of it to us the price of something of more worth to her. Not so can it ever be in the hands of France: the impetuosity of her temper, the energy and restlessness of her character, placed in a point of eternal friction with us, and our character, which, though quiet and loving peace and the pursuit of wealth, is high-minded, despising wealth in competition with insult or injury, enterprising and energetic as any nation on earth;

these circumstances render it impossible that France and the United States can continue long friends, when they meet in so irritable a position. They, as well as we, must be blind if they do not see this; and we must be very improvident if we do not begin to make arrangements on that hypothesis. The day that France takes possession of New Orleans, fixes the sentence which is to restrain her forever within her low-water mark. It seals the union of two nations, who, in conjunction, can maintain exclusive possession of the ocean. From that moment, we must marry ourselves to the British fleet and nation. We must turn all our attention to a maritime force, for which our resources place us on a very high ground, and having formed and connected together a power which may render reinforcement of her settlements here impossible to France, make the first cannon that shall be fired in Europe the signal for tearing up any settlement she may have made, and for holding the two continents of America in sequestration for the common purposes of the United British and American nations. This is not a state of things we seek or desire.

T. Paterson and D. Merrill, *Major Problems in American Foreign Relations*, vol. I: *To 1920*
(Lexington, MA: D. C. Heath, 1995), pp. 100–102.

DOCUMENT 5   SAMUEL WHITE: OPPOSITION TO THE LOUISIANA PURCHASE, 1803

Some Federalists expressed opposition to the Louisiana Purchase on several grounds. However, sensing the popularity of the acquisition, their opposition soon died down. In the following extract from the debates in Congress, Samuel White, a Federalist representative from Delaware, raises questions about the purchase.

November 2, 1803

Mr. [Samuel] White [Delaware] rose and made the following remarks:

Admitting then, Mr. President, that His Catholic Majesty [the King of Spain] is hostile to the cession of this territory to the United States, and no honorable gentleman will deny it, what reasons have we to suppose that the French prefect, provided the Spaniards should interfere, can give to us peaceable possession of the country? He is acknowledged there in no public character, is clothed with no authority, nor has he a single soldier to enforce his orders. I speak now, sir, from mere probabilities. I wish not to be understood as predicting that the French will not cede to us the actual and quiet possession of the territory. I hope to God they may, for possession of it we must have; I mean of New Orleans, and of such other positions on the Mississippi as may be necessary to secure to us forever the complete and uninterrupted navigation of that river.

This I have ever been in favor of; I think it essential to the peace of the United States and to the prosperity of our western country. But as to Louisiana, this new, immense, unbounded world, if it should ever be incorporated into this Union, which I have no idea can be done but by altering the Constitution, I believe it will be the greatest curse that could at present befall us; it may be productive of innumerable evils, and especially of one that I fear even to look upon. Gentlemen on all sides, with very few exceptions, agree that the settlement of this country will be highly injurious and dangerous to the United States; but as to what has been suggested of removing the Creeks and other nations of Indians from the eastern to the western banks of the Mississippi, and of making the fertile regions of Louisiana a howling wilderness, never to be trodden by the foot of civilized man, it is impracticable.

The gentleman from Tennessee (Mr. Cocke) has shown his usual candor on this subject, and I believe with him (to use his strong language) that you had as well pretend to inhibit the fish from swimming in the sea as to prevent the population of that country after its sovereignty shall become ours. To every man acquainted with the adventurous, roving, and enterprising temper of our people, and with the manner in which our western country has been settled, such an idea must be chimerical. The inducements will be so strong that it will be impossible to restrain our citizens from crossing the river. Louisiana must and will become settled if we hold it, and with the very population that would otherwise occupy part of our present territory. Thus our citizens will be removed to the immense distance of 2,000 or 3,000 miles from the capital of the Union, where they will scarcely ever feel the rays of the general government; they will form other commercial connections, and our interests will become distinct.

These, with other causes that human wisdom may not now foresee, will in time effect a separation, and I fear our bounds will be fixed nearer to our houses than the waters of the Mississippi. We have already territory enough, and when I contemplate the evils that may arise to these states from this intended incorporation of Louisiana into the Union, I would rather see it given to France, to Spain, or to any other nation of the earth upon the mere condition that no citizen of the United States should ever settle within its limits, than to see the territory sold for $100,000,000 and we retain the sovereignty.

Selected Readings on Great Issues in American History, 1620–1968 (Encyclopaedia Britannica Educational Corporation, 1969), pp. C5–C6.

DOCUMENT 6   THOMAS JEFFERSON'S INSTRUCTIONS TO MERIWETHER LEWIS, 1803

Jefferson made very detailed plans for the Lewis and Clark expedition. Reading them, one senses he may well have wished to go himself. This is an excerpt from his instructions to one of the leaders of the expedition.

[June 20, 1803]

The object of your mission is to explore the Missouri River, and such principal stream of it, as by its course and communication with the water of the Pacific Ocean, may offer the most direct and practicable water communication across this continent, for the purposes of commerce.

Beginning at the mouth of the Missouri, you will take observations of latitude and longitude of all remarkable points on the river, and especially at the mouths of rivers, at rapids, at islands, and other places and objects distinguished by such natural marks and characters of a durable kind, as that they may with certainty be recognized hereafter. The courses of the river between these points of observation may be supplied by the compass, the logline, and by time, corrected by the observations themselves. The variations of the compass, too, in different places should be noticed.

The interesting points of the portage between the heads of the Missouri and the water offering the best communication with the Pacific Ocean should be fixed by observation and the course of that water to the ocean, in the same manner as that of the Missouri.

Your observations are to be taken with great pains and accuracy, to be entered distinctly and intelligibly for others as well as yourself to comprehend all the elements necessary, with the aid of the usual tables to fix the latitude and longitude of the places at which they were taken, and are to be rendered to the War Office for the purpose of having the calculations made concurrently by proper persons within the U.S. Several copies of these, as well as your other notes, should be made at leisure times and put into the care of the most trustworthy of your attendants, to guard by multiplying them against the accidental losses to which they will be exposed. A further guard would be that one of these copies be written on the paper of the birch, as less liable to injury from damp than common paper.

Selected Readings on Great Issues in American History, 1620–1968 (Encyclopaedia Britannica Educational Corporation, 1969), pp. C4–C5.

DOCUMENT 7   THE MONROE DOCTRINE, 1823

While perhaps not directly connected to American expansionism, the Monroe Doctrine did serve notice that the US would not passively tolerate the expansion of other powers in the Western Hemisphere. President James Monroe announced the Doctrine, which was largely the work of his Secretary of State, John Quincy Adams, in his address to Congress, 2 December 1823.

The citizens of the United States cherish sentiments the most friendly in favor of the liberty and happiness of their fellow-men on that side of the Atlantic. In the wars of the European powers in matters relating to themselves we have never taken any part, nor does it comport with our policy to do so. It is only when our rights are invaded or seriously menaced that we resent injuries or make preparation for our defense. With the movements in this hemisphere we are of necessity more immediately connected, and by causes which must be obvious to all enlightened and impartial observers. ... We owe it, therefore, to candor and to the amicable relations existing between the United States and those powers to declare that we should consider any attempt on their part to extend their system to any portion of this hemisphere as dangerous to our peace and safety. With the existing colonies or dependencies of any European power we have not interfered and shall not interfere. But with the Governments who have declared their independence and maintain it, and whose independence we have, on great consideration and on just principles, acknowledged, we could not view any interposition for the purpose of oppressing them, or controlling in any other manner their destiny, by any European power in any other light than as the manifestation of an unfriendly disposition toward the United States. In the war between those new Governments and Spain we declared our neutrality at the time of their recognition, and to this we have adhered, and shall continue to adhere, provided no change shall occur which, in the judgement of the competent authorities of this Government, shall make a corresponding change on the part of the United States indispensable to their security.

Our policy in regard to Europe, which was adopted at an early stage of the wars which have so long agitated that quarter of the globe, nevertheless remains the same, which is, not to interfere in the internal concerns of any of its powers; to consider the government de facto as the legitimate government for us; to cultivate friendly relations with it, and to preserve those relations by a frank, firm, and manly policy, meeting in all instances the just claims of every power, submitting to injuries from none. But in regard to those continents circumstances are eminently and conspicuously different. It is impossible that the allied powers should extend their political system to any portion of either continent without endangering our peace and happiness; nor can anyone believe that our southern brethren, if left to themselves, would adopt it of their own accord. It is equally impossible, therefore, that we should behold such interposition in any form with indifference. If we look to the comparative strength and resources of Spain and those new Governments, and their distance from each other, it must be obvious that she can never subdue them. It is still the true policy of the United States to leave the parties to themselves, in hope that other powers will pursue the same course ... .

> *The Annals of America*, vol. 5, 1821–1832, *Steps Toward Equalitarianism* (Chicago: Encyclopaedia Britannica, 1968), pp. 74–5.

DOCUMENT 8   ANDREW JACKSON ON INDIAN REMOVAL, 1830

The Indian Removal Bill was passed with Jackson's strong support in May 1830, prompting much debate and criticism. In his annual message to Congress the following December, Jackson defended the policy.

Humanity has often wept over the fate of the aborigines of this country, and philanthropy has been long busily employed in devising means to avert it, but its progress has never for a moment been arrested, and one by one have many powerful tribes disappeared from the earth. To follow to the tomb the last of his race and to tread on the graves of extinct nations excite melancholy reflections. But true philanthropy reconciles the mind to these vicissitudes as it does to the extinction of one generation to make room for another. In the monuments and fortresses of an unknown people, spread over the extensive regions of the West, we behold the memorials of a once powerful race, which was exterminated or has disappeared to make room for the existing savage tribes. Nor is there anything in this which, upon a comprehensive view of the general interests of the human race, is to be regretted. Philanthropy could not wish to see this continent restored to the condition in which it was found by our forefathers. What good man would prefer a country covered with forests and ranged by a few thousand savages to our extensive republic, studded with cities, towns, and prosperous farms, embellished with all the improvements which art can devise or industry execute, occupied by more than 12,000,000 happy people, and filled with all the blessings of liberty, civilization, and religion?

The present policy of the government is but a continuation of the same progressive change by a milder process. The tribes which occupied the countries now constituting the Eastern states were annihilated or have melted away to make room for the whites. The waves of population and civilization are rolling to the westward, and we now propose to acquire the countries occupied by red men of the South and West by a fair exchange, and, at the expense of the United States, to send them to a land where their existence may be prolonged and perhaps made perpetual.

Doubtless it will be painful to leave the graves of their fathers; but what do they more than our ancestors did or than our children are now doing? To better their condition in an unknown land our forefathers left all that was dear in earthly objects. Our children by thousands yearly leave the land of their birth to seek new homes in distant regions. Does humanity weep at these painful separations from everything, animate and inanimate, with which the young heart has become entwined? Far from it. It is rather a source of joy that our country affords scope where our young population may range unconstrained in body or in mind, developing the power and faculties of man in their highest perfection. These remove hundreds and almost thousands of miles at their own expense, purchase the lands they occupy, and support themselves at their new homes from the moment of their arrival. Can it be cruel in this government when, by events which it cannot control, the Indian is made discontented in his ancient home to purchase his lands, to give him a new and extensive territory, to pay the expense of his removal, and support him a year in his new abode? How many thousands of our own people would gladly embrace the opportunity of removing to the West on such conditions? If the offer made to the Indians were extended to them, they would be hailed with gratitude and joy.

And is it supposed that the wandering savage has a stronger attachment to his home than the settled, civilized Christian? Is it more afflicting to him to leave the graves of his fathers than it is to our brothers and children? Rightly considered, the policy of the general government toward the red man is not only liberal but generous. He is unwilling to submit to the laws of the states and mingle with their population. To save him from this alternative, or perhaps utter annihilation, the general government kindly offers him a new home and proposes to pay the whole expense of his removal and settlement.

Selected Readings on Great Issues in American History, 1620–1968 (Encyclopaedia Britannica Educational Corporation, 1969), pp. C10–C11.

DOCUMENT 9   **APPEAL OF THE CHEROKEE NATION, 1830**

When the Removal Bill was passed on 28 May 1830, the Cherokee Nation addressed another appeal (or memorial), this time to the 'People of the United States,' reminding them and their government of the existing obligations resulting from the treaties that had been agreed to between the two nations.

We are aware, that some persons suppose it will be for our advantage to remove beyond the Mississippi. We think otherwise. Our people universally think otherwise. Thinking that it would be fatal to their interests, they have almost to a man sent their memorial to congress deprecating the necessity of a removal. This question was distinctly before their minds when they signed their memorial. ...

We wish to remain on the land of our fathers. We have a perfect and original right to remain without interruption or molestation. The treaties with us, and laws of the United States made in pursuance of treaties, guaranty our residence and our privileges, and secure us against intruders. Our only request is, that these treaties may be fulfilled, and these laws executed.

But if we are compelled to leave our country, we see nothing but ruin before us. The country west of the Arkansas territory is unknown to us. From what we can learn of it, we have no prepossessions in its favor. All the inviting parts of it, as we believe, are preoccupied by various Indian nations, to which it has been assigned. They would regard us as intruders, and look upon us with an evil eye. The far greater part of that region is, beyond all controversy, badly supplied with wood and water; and no Indian tribe can live as agriculturists without these articles. All our neighbors, in case of our removal, though crowded into our near vicinity; would speak a language totally different from ours, and practice different customs. The original possessors of that region are now wandering savages lurking for prey in the neighborhood. They have always been at war, and would be easily tempted to turn their arms against peaceful emigrants. Were the country to which we are urged much better than it is represented to be, and were it free from the objections which we have made to it, still it is not the land of our birth, nor of our affections. It contains neither the scenes of our childhood, nor the graves of our fathers. ...

We have been called a poor, ignorant, and degraded people. We certainly are not rich; nor have we ever boasted of our knowledge, or our moral or intellectual elevation. But there is not a man within our limits so ignorant as not to know that he has the right to live on the land of his fathers, in the possession of his immemorial privileges, and that this right has been acknowledged and guaranteed by the United States; nor is there a man so degraded as not to feel a keen sense of injury, on being deprived of this right and driven into exile.

It is under a sense of the most pungent feelings that we make this, perhaps our last appeal to the good people of the United States. It cannot be that the community we are addressing, remarkable for its intelligence and religious sensibilities, and pre-eminent for its devotion to the rights of man, will lay aside this appeal, without considering that we stand in need of its sympathy and commiseration. We know that to the Christian and to the philanthropist the voice of our multiplied sorrows and fiery trials will not appear as an idle tale. In our own land, on our own soil, and in our own dwellings, which we reared for our wives and for our little ones, when there was peace on our mountains and in our valleys, we are encountering troubles which cannot but try our very souls.

But shall we, on account of these troubles, forsake our beloved country? Shall we be compelled by a civilized and Christian people, with whom we have lived in perfect peace for the last forty years, and for whom we have willingly bled in war, to bid a final adieu to our homes, our farms, our streams and our beautiful forests? No. We are still firm. We intend still to cling, with our wonted affection, to the land which gave us birth, and which, every day of our lives, brings to us new and stronger ties of attachment. We appeal to the judge of all the earth, who will finally award us justice, and to the good sense of the American people, whether we are intruders upon the land of others. Our consciences bear us witness that we are the invaders of no man's rights – we have robbed no man of his territory – we have usurped no man's authority, nor have we deprived any one of his unalienable privileges. How then shall we indirectly confess the right of another people to our land by leaving it forever? On the soil which contains the ashes of our beloved men we wish to live – on this soil we wish to die.

We intreat those to whom the foregoing paragraphs are addressed, to remember the great law of love. 'Do to others as ye would that others should do to you' – Let them remember that of all nations on the earth, they are under the greatest obligation to obey this law. We pray them to remember that, for the sake of principle, their forefathers were compelled to leave, therefore driven from the old world, and that the winds of persecution wafted them over the great waters and landed them on the shores of the new world, when the Indian was the sole lord and proprietor of these extensive domains – Let them remember in what way they were received by the savage of America, when power was in his hand, and his ferocity could not be restrained by any human arm. We urge them to bear in mind, that those who would now ask of them a cup of cold water, and a spot of earth, a portion of their own patrimonial possessions, on which to live and die in peace, are the descendants of those, whose origin, as inhabitants of North America, history and tradition are alike insufficient to reveal. Let them bring to remembrance all these facts, and they cannot, and we are sure, they will not fail to remember, and sympathize with us in these our trials and sufferings.

F. Binder and D. Reimers (eds), *The Way We Lived: Essays and Documents in American Social History*, vol. I, *1492 to 1877*, 4th edn (Boston: Houghton-Mifflin, 2000), pp. 161–2.

When the settlers in Texas revolted against Mexican control, they wrote a declaration of independence, modeled in some fashion after the US Declaration, listing their grievances against the Mexican government and seeking to justify their actions.

Unanimous Declaration of Independence, of the Delegates of the People of Texas, in General Convention, at the Town of Washington, on the Second Day of March, 1836.

When a government has ceased to protect the lives, liberty and property of the people, from whom its legitimate powers are derived, and for the advancement of whose happiness it was instituted, and so far from being a guarantee for the enjoyment of those inestimable and inalienable rights, becomes an instrument in the hands of evil rulers for their oppression ...

When, long after the spirit of the constitution has departed, moderation is at length so far lost by those in power, that even the semblance of freedom is removed, and the forms themselves of the constitution discontinued, and so far from their petitions and remonstrances being regarded, the agents who bear them are thrown into dungeons, and mercenary armies sent forth to force a new government upon them at the point of the bayonet.

When, in consequence of such acts of malfeasance and abdication on the part of the government, anarchy prevails, and civil society is dissolved into its original elements. In such a crisis, the first law of nature, the right of self-preservation, the inherent and inalienable rights of the people to appeal to first principles, and take their political affairs into their own hands in extreme cases, enjoins it as a right towards themselves, and a sacred obligation to their posterity, to abolish such government, and create another in its stead, calculated to rescue them from impending dangers, and to secure their future welfare and happiness.

Nations, as well as individuals, are amenable for their acts to the public opinion of mankind. A statement of a part of our grievances is therefore submitted to an impartial world, in justification of the hazardous but unavoidable step now taken, of severing our political connection with the Mexican people, and assuming an independent attitude among the nations of the earth.

The Mexican government, by its colonization laws, invited and induced the Anglo-American population of Texas to colonize its wilderness under the pledged faith of a written constitution, that they should continue to enjoy that constitutional liberty and republican government to which they had been habituated in the land of their birth, the United States of America.

In this expectation they have been cruelly disappointed, inasmuch as the Mexican nation has acquiesced in the late changes made in the government by General Antonio Lopez de Santa Anna, who having overturned the constitution of his country, now offers us the cruel alternative, either to abandon our homes, acquired by so many privations, or submit to the most intolerable of all tyranny, the combined despotism of the sword and the priesthood. ...

It incarcerated in a dungeon, for a long time, one of our citizens, for no other cause but a zealous endeavor to procure the acceptance of our constitution, and the establishment of a state government.

It has failed and refused to secure, on a firm basis, the right of trial by jury, that palladium of civil liberty, and only safe guarantee for the life, liberty, and property of the citizen. ...

It has suffered the military commandants, stationed among us, to exercise arbitrary acts of oppression and tyranny, thus trampling upon the most sacred rights of the citizens, and rendering the military superior to the civil power.

It has dissolved, by force of arms, the state Congress of Coahuila and Texas, and obliged our representatives to fly for their lives from the seat of government, thus depriving us of the fundamental political right of representation.

It has demanded the surrender of a number of our citizens, and ordered military detachments to seize and carry them into the Interior for trial, in contempt of the civil authorities, and in defiance of the laws and the constitution.

It has made piratical attacks upon our commerce, by commissioning foreign desperadoes, and authorizing them to seize our vessels, and convey the property of our citizens to far distant ports for confiscation.

It denies us the right of worshipping the Almighty according to the dictates of our own conscience, by the support of a national religion, calculated to promote the temporal interest of its human functionaries, rather than the glory of the true and living God.

It has demanded us to deliver up our arms, which are essential to our defense, the rightful property of freemen, and formidable only to tyrannical governments.

It has invaded our country both by sea and by land, with intent to lay waste our territory, and drive us from our homes; and has now a large mercenary army advancing, to carry on against us a war of extermination.

It has, through its emissaries, incited the merciless savage, with the tomahawk and scalping knife, to massacre the inhabitants of our defenseless frontiers.

It hath been, during the whole time of our connection with it, the contemptible sport and victim of successive military revolutions, and hath continually exhibited every characteristic of a weak, corrupt, and tyrannical government.

These, and other grievances, were patiently borne by the people of Texas, until they reached that point at which forbearance ceases to be a virtue. We then took up arms in defense of the national constitution. We appealed to our Mexican brethren for assistance. Our appeal has been made in vain. Though months have elapsed, no sympathetic response has yet been heard from the Interior. We are, therefore, forced to the melancholy conclusion, that the Mexican people have acquiesced in the destruction of their liberty, and the substitution therfor of a military government; that they are unfit to be free, and incapable of self government.

The necessity of self-preservation, therefore, now decrees our eternal political separation. We, therefore, the delegates with plenary powers of the people of Texas, in solemn convention assembled, appealing to a candid world for the necessities of our condition, do hereby resolve and declare, that our political connection with the Mexican nation has forever ended, and that the people of Texas do now constitute a free, Sovereign, and independent republic, and are fully invested with all the rights and attributes which properly belong to independent nations; and, conscious of the rectitude of our intentions, we fearlessly and confidently commit the issue to the decision of the Supreme arbiter of the destinies of nations.

D. Davis and S. Mintz (eds), *The Boisterous Sea of Liberty: A Documentary History of America From Discovery Through the Civil War* (New York: Oxford University Press, 1998), p. 407.

DOCUMENT 11   JOHN C. CALHOUN ON EXPANSION INTO THE NORTHWEST, 1843

In December 1841, a bill was introduced into Congress calling for the erection of fortifications in the Oregon country, which would have abrogated the Joint Occupancy Treaty between the US and Great Britain. John C. Calhoun, Senator from South Carolina, spoke in January 1843 to oppose this bill. He believed no such action was needed, because Oregon would inevitably come to be part of the United States.

Time is acting for us; and if we shall have the wisdom to trust its operation, it will assert and maintain our right with restless force, without costing a cent of money or a drop of blood. There is, often, in the affairs of government, more efficiency and wisdom in nonaction than in action. All we want to effect our object in this case is 'a wise and masterly inactivity.'

Our population is rolling toward the shores of the Pacific with an impetus greater than we realize. It is one of those forward movements which leaves anticipation behind. In the period of thirty-two years which have elapsed since I took my seat in the other house, the Indian frontier has receded 1,000 miles to the West. At that time our population was much less than half what it is now. It was then increasing at the rate of about 250,000 annually; it is now not less than 600,000, and still increasing at the rate of something more than 3 percent compound annually. At that rate, it will soon reach the yearly increase of 1 million.

If to this be added that the region west of Arkansas and the state of Missouri, and south of the Missouri River, is occupied by half civilized tribes, who have their lands secured to them by treaty (and which will prevent the spread of population in that direction), and that this great and increasing tide will be forced to take the comparatively narrow channel to the north of that river and south of our northern boundary, some conception may be formed of the strength with which the current will run in that direction and how soon it will reach the eastern gorges of the Rocky Mountains. I say some conception, for I feel assured that the reality will outrun the anticipation. ...

Such is the wonderful growth of a population which has attained the number ours has, yearly increasing at a compound rate, and such the impetus with which it is forcing its way, resistlessly, westward. It will soon, far sooner than anticipated, reach the Rocky Mountains and be ready to pour into the Oregon territory, when it will come into our possession without resistance or struggle; or, if there should be resistance, it would be feeble and ineffectual.

We should then be as much stronger there, comparatively, as she is now stronger than we are; and it would then be as idle to assert and maintain her exclusive claim to the territory against us as it would now be in us to attempt it against her. Let us be wise and abide our time; and it will accomplish all that we desire with more certainty and with infinitely less sacrifice than we can without it.

Annals of America, vol. 7, *Manifest Destiny* (Chicago: Encyclopaedia Britannica, 1968), pp. 87–8.

DOCUMENT 12   JAMES K. POLK'S INAUGURAL ADDRESS, 1845

Polk campaigned in 1844 on 'the re-occupation of Oregon and the re-annexation of Texas,' implying that the United States at one time had a clear title to these regions. In his inaugural address, he promised quick action to see these areas added to the national domain.

Tuesday, March 4, 1845

Fellow-Citizens:

Without solicitation on my part, I have been chosen by the free and voluntary suffrages of my countrymen to the most honorable and most responsible office on earth. I am deeply impressed with gratitude for the confidence reposed in me. Honored with this distinguished consideration at an earlier period of life than any of my predecessors, I can not disguise the diffidence with which I am about to enter on the discharge of my official duties. ...

The inestimable value of our Federal Union is felt and acknowledged by all. By this system of united and confederated States our people are permitted collectively and individually to seek their own happiness in their own way, and the consequences have been most auspicious. Since the Union was formed the number of the States has increased from thirteen to twenty-eight; two of these have taken their position as members of the Confederacy within the last week. Our population has increased from three to twenty millions. New communities and States are seeking protection under its aegis, and multitudes from the Old World are flocking to our shores to participate in its blessings. Beneath its benign sway peace and prosperity prevail. Freed from the burdens and miseries of war, our trade and intercourse have extended throughout the world. ...

These are some of the blessings secured to our happy land by our Federal Union. To perpetuate them it is our sacred duty to preserve it. Who shall assign limits to the achievements of free minds and free hands under the protection of this glorious Union?...

The Republic of Texas has made known her desire to come into our Union, to form a part of our Confederacy and enjoy with us the blessings of liberty secured and guaranteed by our Constitution. Texas was once a part of our country – was unwisely ceded away to a foreign power – is now independent, and possesses an undoubted right to dispose of a part or the whole of her territory and to merge her sovereignty as a separate and independent state in ours. I congratulate my country that by an act of the late Congress of the United States the assent of this Government has been given to the reunion, and it only remains for the two countries to agree upon the terms to consummate an object so important to both.

I regard the question of annexation as belonging exclusively to the United States and Texas. They are independent powers competent to contract, and foreign nations have no right to interfere with them or to take exceptions to their reunion. Foreign powers do not seem to appreciate the true character of our Government. Our Union is a confederation of independent States, whose policy is peace with each other and all the world. To enlarge its limits is to extend the dominions of peace over additional territories and increasing millions. The world has nothing to fear from military ambition in our Government. While the Chief Magistrate and the popular branch of Congress are elected for short terms by the suffrages of those millions who must in their own persons bear all the burdens and miseries of war, our Government can not be otherwise than pacific. Foreign powers should therefore look on the annexation of Texas to the United States not as the conquest of a nation seeking to extend her dominions by arms and violence, but as the peaceful acquisition of a territory once her own, by adding another member to our confederation, with the consent of that member, thereby diminishing the chances of war and opening to them new and ever-increasing markets for their products.

To Texas the reunion is important, because the strong protecting arm of our Government would be extended over her, and the vast resources of her fertile soil and genial climate would be speedily developed, while the safety of New Orleans and of our whole southwestern frontier against hostile aggression, as well as the interests of the whole Union, would be promoted by it.

In the earlier stages of our national existence the opinion prevailed with some that our system of confederated States could not operate successfully over an extended territory, and serious objections have at different times been made to the enlargement of our boundaries. These objections were earnestly urged when we acquired Louisiana. Experience has shown that they were not well founded. The title of numerous Indian tribes to vast tracts of country has been extinguished; new States have been admitted into the Union; new Territories have been created and our jurisdiction and laws extended over them. As our population has expanded, the Union has been cemented and strengthened. As our boundaries have been enlarged and our agricultural population has been spread over a large surface, our federative system has acquired additional strength and security. It may well be doubted whether it would not be in greater danger of overthrow if our present population were confined to the comparatively narrow limits of the original thirteen States than it is now that they are sparsely settled over a more expanded territory. It is confidently believed that our system may be safely extended to the utmost bounds of our territorial limits, and that as it shall be extended the bonds of our Union, so far from being weakened, will become stronger. ...

Nor will it become in a less degree my duty to assert and maintain by all constitutional means the right of the United States to that portion of our territory which lies beyond the Rocky Mountains. Our title to the country of the Oregon is 'clear and unquestionable,' and already are our people preparing to perfect that title by occupying it with their wives and children. But eighty years ago our population was confined on the west by the ridge of the Alleghenies. Within that period – within the lifetime, I might say, of some of my hearers – our people, increasing to many millions, have filled the eastern valley of the Mississippi, adventurously ascended the Missouri to its headsprings, and are already engaged in establishing the blessings of self-government in valleys of which the rivers flow to the Pacific. The world beholds the peaceful triumphs of the industry of our emigrants. To us belongs the duty of protecting them adequately wherever they may be upon our soil. The jurisdiction of our laws and the benefits of our republican institutions should be extended over them in the distant regions which they have selected for their homes. The increasing facilities of intercourse will easily bring the States, of which the formation in that part of our territory can not be long delayed, within the sphere of our federative Union. In the meantime every obligation imposed by treaty or conventional stipulations should be sacredly respected.

http:www.yale.edu/lawweb/avalon/presiden/inaug/polk.htm

> DOCUMENT 13   **JOHN L. O'SULLIVAN ON MANIFEST DESTINY, 1845**

Although many had used various terms to mean virtually the same thing, the phrase 'manifest destiny' was coined by John L. O'Sullivan in an article urging the annexation of Texas in July 1845, in the United States Magazine and Democratic Review.

Annexation

It is time now for opposition to the annexation of Texas to cease, all further agitation of the waters of bitterness and strife, at least in connection with this question, even though it may perhaps be required of us as a necessary condition of the freedom of our institutions, that we must live on forever in a state of unpausing struggle and excitement upon some subject of party division or other. But, in regard to Texas, enough has now been given to party. It is time for the common duty of patriotism to the country to succeed; or if this claim will not be recognized, it is at least time for common sense to acquiesce with decent grace in the inevitable and the irrevocable.

Texas is now ours. Already, before these words are written, her convention has undoubtedly ratified the acceptance, by her congress, of our proffered invitation into the Union; and made the requisite changes in her already republican form of constitution to adapt it to its future federal relations. Her star and her stripe may already be said to have taken their place in the glorious blazon of our common nationality; and the sweep of our eagle's wing already includes within its circuit the wide extent of her fair and fertile land. ...

Why, were other reasoning wanting, in favor of now elevating this question of the reception of Texas into the Union, out of the lower region of our past party dissensions, up to its proper level of a high and broad nationality, it surely is to be found, found abundantly, in the manner in which other nations have undertaken to intrude themselves into it, between us and the proper parties to the case, in a spirit of hostile interference against us, for the avowed object of thwarting our policy and hampering our power, limiting our greatness and checking the fulfillment of our manifest destiny to overspread the continent allotted by Providence for the free development of our yearly multiplying millions. This we have seen done by England, our old rival and enemy; and by France, strangely coupled with her against us, under the influence of the Anglicism strongly tinging [*sic*] the policy of her present prime minister, Guizot. ...

It is wholly untrue, and unjust to ourselves, the pretense that the annexation has been a measure of spoliation, unrightful and unrighteous – of military conquest under forms of peace and law – of territorial aggrandizement at the expense of justice, and justice due by a double sanctity to the weak. This view of the question is wholly unfounded, and has been before so amply refuted in these pages, as well as in a thousand others modes, that we shall not again dwell upon it.

Annals of America, vol. 7, *Manifest Destiny* (Chicago: Encyclopaedia Britannica, 1968), pp. 288–92.

DOCUMENT 14   JAMES K. POLK'S WAR MESSAGE, 1846

When President Polk appeared before Congress in May 1846, he did not ask for a declaration of war, but charged that a state of war existed by the actions of Mexico.

Washington, May 11, 1846

To the Senate and House of Representatives: The existing state of the relations between the United States and Mexico renders it proper that I should bring the subject to the consideration of Congress. In my message at the commencement of your present session the state of these relations; the causes which led to the suspension of diplomatic intercourse between the two countries in March, 1845, and the long-continued and unredressed wrongs and injuries committed by the Mexican Government on citizens of the United States in their persons and property were briefly set forth. ...

In my message at the commencement of the present session I informed you that upon the earnest appeal both of the Congress and convention of Texas I had ordered an efficient military force to take a position 'between the Nueces and the Del Norte.' This had become necessary to meet a threatened invasion of Texas by the Mexican forces, for which extensive military preparations had been made. The invasion was threatened solely because Texas had determined, in accordance with a solemn resolution of the Congress of the United States, to annex herself to our Union, and under these circumstances it was plainly our duty to extend our protection over her citizens and soil.

This force was concentrated at Corpus Christi, and remained there until after I had received such information from Mexico as rendered it probable, if not certain, that the Mexican Government would refuse to receive our envoy. Meantime Texas, by the final action of our Congress, had become an integral part of our Union. The Congress of Texas, by its act of December 19, 1836, had declared the Rio del Norte to be the boundary of that Republic. Its jurisdiction had been extended and exercised beyond the Nueces. The country between that river and the Del Norte had been represented in the Congress and in the convention of Texas, had thus taken part in the act of annexation itself, and is now included within one of our Congressional districts. Our own Congress had, moreover, with great unanimity, by the act approved December 31, 1845, recognized the country beyond the Nueces as a part of our territory by including it within our own revenue system, and a revenue officer to reside within that district has been appointed by and with the advice and consent of the Senate. It became, therefore, of urgent necessity to provide for the defense of that portion of our country. ...

The Army moved from Corpus Christi on the 11th of March, and on the 28th of that month arrived on the left bank of the Del Norte opposite to Matamoras, where it encamped on a commanding position, which has since been strengthened by the erection of fieldworks. ...

The Mexican forces at Matamoras assumed a belligerent attitude, and on the 12th of April General Ampudia, then in command, notified General Taylor to break up his camp within twenty-four hours and to retire beyond the Nueces River, and in the event of his failure to comply with these demands announced that arms, and arms alone, must decide the question. But no open act of hostility was committed until the 14th of April. On that day General Arista, who had succeeded to the command of the Mexican forces, communicated to General Taylor that 'he considered hostilities commenced and should prosecute them.' A party of dragoons of 63 men and officers were on the same day dispatched from the American camp up the Rio del Norte, on its left bank, to ascertain whether the Mexican troops had crossed or were preparing to cross the river, 'became engaged with a large body of these troops, and after a short affair, in which some 16 were killed and wounded, appear to have been surrounded and compelled to surrender.' The grievous wrongs perpetrated by Mexico upon our citizens throughout a long period of years remain unredressed, and solemn treaties pledging her public faith for this redress have been disregarded. A government either unable or unwilling to enforce the execution of such treaties fails to perform one of its plainest duties. ...

The cup of forbearance had been exhausted even before the recent information from the frontier of the Del Norte. But now, after reiterated menaces, Mexico has passed the boundary of the United States, has invaded our territory and shed American blood upon the American soil. She has proclaimed that hostilities have commenced, and that the two nations are now at war.

As war exists, and, notwithstanding all our efforts to avoid it, exists by the act of Mexico herself, we are called upon by every consideration of duty and patriotism to vindicate with decision the honor, the rights, and the interests of our country. ...

In further vindication of our rights and defense of our territory, I involve the prompt action of Congress to recognize the existence of the war, and to place at the disposition of the Executive the means of prosecuting the war with vigor, and thus hastening the restoration of peace. To this end I recommend that authority should be given to call into the public service a large body of volunteers to serve for not less than six or twelve months unless sooner discharged. A volunteer force is beyond question more efficient than any other description of citizen soldiers, and it is not to be doubted that a number far beyond that required would readily rush to the field upon the call of their country. I further recommend that a liberal provision be made for sustaining our entire military force and furnishing it with supplies and munitions of war.

The most energetic and prompt measures and the immediate appearance in arms of a large and overpowering force are recommended to Congress as the most certain and efficient means of bringing the existing collision with Mexico to a speedy and successful termination.

In making these recommendations I deem it proper to declare that it is my anxious desire not only to terminate hostilities speedily, but to bring all matters in dispute between this Government and Mexico to an early and amicable adjustment; and in this view I shall be prepared to renew negotiations whenever Mexico shall be ready to receive propositions or to make propositions of her own.

I transmit herewith a copy of the correspondence between our envoy to Mexico and the Mexican minister for foreign affairs, and so much of the correspondence between that envoy and the Secretary of State and between the Secretary of War and the general in command on the Del Norte as is necessary to a full understanding of the subject.

James K. Polk

http://www.yale.edu/lawweb/avalon/presiden/messages/polk01.htm

DOCUMENT 15   EMIGRATION TO CALIFORNIA, 1846

Even before the gold rush which began in 1849, the climate and bountiful prospects for agriculture were bringing large numbers of emigrants to California. This account from an early newspaper published in California describes the arrival of the emigrants.

Emigrants from the United States are daily flocking into California, their landmark, after crossing the Rocky Mountains, is the Sacramento valley, amongst them are mechanics and labourers of all descriptions, and altho' they invariably strike for the Sacramento valley, still not one half of them will settle there, they will as soon as they get acquainted with the country, and the winter season is over, spread over all California, and as many of these are people who understand agriculture in all its branches, they will undoubtedly spy out thousands of acres of land, which are now considered useless, except for grazing, and will in a short time prove to the old inhabitants that there is more land fit for cultivation in California, than ever has been imagined, by the natives; and many vegetable substances will be planted, and brought to maturity, which heretofore have never had a fair trial.

'Emigration,' Monterey *Californian*, 7 November 1846. Reprinted in F. Binder and
D. Reimers (eds), *The Way We Lived: Essays and Documents in American Social History*
(Boston: Houghton-Mifflin, 2000), p. 182.

DOCUMENT 16   EMIGRATION TO OREGON, 1847

Reports of emigrants who went overland to the Far West were important in stimulating the desire of others to emigrate. They often understated the dangers and challenges, and overstated the benefits and conditions in their new homelands.

April 6, 1847

We arrived in Oregon City on the 12th of September last. We reached Fort Laramie in 42 days from Independence; Fort Hall in 33 days more; the Dalles in 37 days more, and Oregon City in 16 days more – making in all 128 days. Our journey was two weeks longer than necessary had we lost no time. We met with no serious obstacles on our journey. We had to raise the front of our wagon beds two or three inches in crossing the Laramie Fork to keep the water out; sometimes we had long drives to find a good place for camping, with water and grass. ... No single man should come to this country. One third of the men in Oregon at this time are without wives. Nothing but men with families are wanted here to till the soil, to make this one of the greatest countries in the world. This country does not get so muddy as Illinois. There is no dust in summer here. The good land in this country is more extensive than I expected to find it. The hills are not so high as represented. From the Cascade mountains to the Pacific, the whole country can be cultivated. The natural soil of this country, especially in the bottoms, is a black loam, mixed with gravel and clay. We have good timber; but there appears to be a scarcity of good building rock. The small streams furnish us with trout the year round. ...

The roads to Oregon are not as bad as represented. Hastings in his history speaks of the Falls of Columbia being 50 feet and roaring loud, making the earth tremble, etc. The falls are about like that of a mill dam. Everything in this country now is high, except molasses, sugar and salt; but when we raise our wheat crop to trade on, we will make them pay for their high charges. I think no place where a living is to be made out of the earth can be preferable to Oregon for that purpose – and let people say what they may – all agree that it is healthy. It is certainly the healthiest country in the world, disease is scarcely known here, except among the late emigrants, ninety-nine out of a hundred of them get well the first season. ...

Richard R. Howard

Letter by Richard R. Howard, 6 April 1847, published in the [Springfield] *Illinois Register,* 11 November 1847. Reprinted in F. Binder and D. Reimers (eds) *The Way We Lived: Essays and Documents in American Social History* (Boston: Houghton-Mifflin, 2000), pp. 182–3.

DOCUMENT 17   **ABRAHAM LINCOLN, 'THE SPOT RESOLUTIONS,' 1847**

Elected as a Whig Congressman from Illinois in 1846, Lincoln used his first speech in the US House to propose a set of resolutions asking President Polk to explain certain items concerning the causes of the Mexican War.

RESOLUTIONS IN THE UNITED STATES HOUSE OF REPRESENTATIVES
December 22, 1847

Whereas, The President of the United States, in his message of May 11, 1846, has declared that 'the Mexican government not only refused to receive him [the envoy of the United States], or to listen to his propositions, but after a long-continued series of menaces, has at last invaded our territory and shed the blood of our fellow-citizens on our own soil.'

And again, in his message of December 8, 1846, that 'we had ample cause of war against Mexico long before the breaking out of hostilities; but even then we forbore to take redress into our own hands until Mexico herself became the aggressor, by invading our soil in hostile array, and shedding the blood of our citizens.'

And yet again, in his message of December 7, 1847, that 'the Mexican Government refused even to hear the terms of adjustment which he [our minister of peace] was authorized to propose, and finally, under wholly unjustifiable pretexts, involved the two countries in war, by invading the territory of the State of Texas, striking the first blow, and shedding the blood of our citizens on our own soil.'

And whereas, This House is desirous to obtain a full knowledge of all the facts which go to establish whether the particular spot on which the blood of our citizens was so shed was or was not at that time our own soil; therefore,

Resolved, By the House of Representatives, that the President of the United States be respectfully requested to inform this House –

First. Whether the spot on which the blood of our citizens was shed, as in his message declared, was or was not within the territory of Spain, at least after the treaty of 1819 until the Mexican revolution.

Second. Whether that spot is or is not within the territory which was wrested from Spain by the revolutionary Government of Mexico.

Third. Whether that spot is or is not within a settlement of people, which settlement has existed ever since long before the Texas revolution, and until its inhabitants fled before the approach of the United States army.

Fourth. Whether that settlement is or is not isolated from any and all other settlements by the Gulf and the Rio Grande on the south and west, and by wide uninhabited regions on the north and east.

Fifth. Whether the people of that settlement, or a majority of them, or any of them, have ever submitted themselves to the government or laws of Texas or of the United States, by consent or by compulsion, either by accepting office, or voting at elections, or paying tax, or serving on juries, or having process served upon them, or in any other way.

Sixth. Whether the people of that settlement did or did not flee from the approach of the United States army, leaving unprotected their homes and their growing crops, *before* the blood was shed, as in the message stated; and whether the first blood, so shed, was or was not shed within the inclosure of one of the people who had thus fled from it.

Seventh. Whether our citizens, whose blood was shed, as in his message declared, were or were not, at that time, armed officers and soldiers, sent into that settlement by the military order of the President, through the Secretary of War.

Eighth. Whether the military force of the United States was or was not so sent into that settlement after General Taylor had more than once intimated to the War Department that, in his opinion, no such movement was necessary to the defense or protection of Texas.

J. Nicolay and J. Hay (eds), *Complete Works of Abraham Lincoln,.* new and expanded edn (New York: Francis D. Tandy, 1905), vol. I, pp. 318–20.

DOCUMENT 18   THE WILMOT PROVISO, 1846

Before the Mexican War was even over, the question of whether any territory taken from Mexico would become slave or free was already haunting Congress. In August 1846, David Wilmot, a congressman from Pennsylvania, introduced this amendment to a war appropriations bill. The Proviso was passed by the US House of Representatives in 1846 and 1847, but never passed by the US Senate.

Provided that, as an express and fundamental condition to the acquisition of any territory from the Republic of Mexico by the United States, by virtue of any treaty which may be negotiated between them, and to the use by the Executive of the moneys herein appropriated, neither slavery nor involuntary servitude shall ever exist in any part of said territory, except for crime, whereof the party shall first be duly convicted.

T. Paterson and D. Merrill, *Major Problems in American Foreign Relations*, vol. I: *To 1920* (Lexington, MA: D. C. Heath, 1995), p. 255.

DOCUMENT 19   THE TREATY OF GUADALUPE HIDALGO, 1848

The Treaty of Guadalupe Hidalgo formally ended the Mexican War, and described the new boundaries between the two nations. These excerpts are taken from the text of the treaty approved by the US Senate and the Mexican government in the summer of 1848.

IN THE NAME OF ALMIGHTY GOD The United States of America and the United Mexican States animated by a sincere desire to put an end to the calamities of the war which unhappily exists between the two Republics and to establish upon a solid basis relations of peace and friendship, which shall confer reciprocal benefits upon the citizens of both, and assure the concord, harmony, and mutual confidence wherein the two people should live, as good neighbors have for that purpose appointed their respective plenipotentiaries, ... Who, after a reciprocal communication of their respective full powers, have, under the protection of Almighty God, the author of peace, arranged, agreed upon, and signed the following:
Treaty of Peace, Friendship, Limits, and Settlement between the United States of America and the Mexican Republic.

ARTICLE I
There shall be firm and universal peace between the United States of America and the Mexican Republic, and between their respective countries, territories, cities, towns, and people, without exception of places or persons.

ARTICLE IV

... The final evacuation of the territory of the Mexican Republic, by the forces of the United States, shall be completed in three months from the said exchange of ratifications, or sooner if possible; the Mexican Government hereby engaging, as in the foregoing article to use all means in its power for facilitating such evacuation, and rendering it convenient to the troops, and for promoting a good understanding between them and the inhabitants.

... All prisoners of war taken on either side, on land or on sea, shall be restored as soon as practicable after the exchange of ratifications of this treaty.

ARTICLE V

The boundary line between the two Republics shall commence in the Gulf of Mexico, three leagues from land, opposite the mouth of the Rio Grande, otherwise called Rio Bravo del Norte, or Opposite the mouth of its deepest branch, if it should have more than one branch emptying directly into the sea; from thence up the middle of that river, following the deepest channel, where it has more than one, to the point where it strikes the southern boundary of New Mexico; thence, westwardly, along the whole southern boundary of New Mexico (which runs north of the town called Paso) to its western termination; thence, northward, along the western line of New Mexico, until it intersects the first branch of the river Gila; ... until it empties into the Rio Colorado; thence across the Rio Colorado, following the division line between Upper and Lower California, to the Pacific Ocean.

...

The boundary line established by this article shall be religiously respected by each of the two republics, and no change shall ever be made therein, except by the express and free consent of both nations, lawfully given by the General Government of each, in conformity with its own constitution.

ARTICLE VIII

Mexicans now established in territories previously belonging to Mexico, and which remain for the future within the limits of the United States, as defined by the present treaty, shall be free to continue where they now reside, or to remove at any time to the Mexican Republic, retaining the property which they possess in the said territories, or disposing thereof, and removing the proceeds wherever they please, without their being subjected, on this account, to any contribution, tax, or charge whatever.

Those who shall prefer to remain in the said territories may either retain the title and rights of Mexican citizens, or acquire those of citizens of the United States. But they shall be under the obligation to make their election within one year from the date of the exchange of ratifications of this treaty; and those who shall remain in the said territories after the expiration of that year, without having declared their intention to retain the character of Mexicans, shall be considered to have elected to become citizens of the United States.

In the said territories, property of every kind, now belonging to Mexicans not established there, shall be inviolably respected. The present owners, the heirs of these, and all Mexicans who may hereafter acquire said property by contract, shall enjoy with respect to it guarantees equally ample as if the same belonged to citizens of the United States.

ARTICLE IX

The Mexicans who, in the territories aforesaid, shall not preserve the character of citizens of the Mexican Republic, conformably with what is stipulated in the preceding article, shall be incorporated into the Union of the United States, and be admitted at the proper time (to be judged of by the Congress of the United States) to the enjoyment of all the rights of citizens of the United States, according to the principles of the Constitution; and in the mean time, shall be maintained and protected in the free enjoyment of their liberty and property, and secured in the free exercise of their religion without restriction.

ARTICLE XII

In consideration of the extension acquired by the boundaries of the United States, as defined in the fifth article of the present treaty, the Government of the United States engages to pay to that of the Mexican Republic the sum of fifteen Millions of dollars. ...

ARTICLE XIII

The United States engage, moreover, to assume and pay to the claimants all the amounts now due them, and those hereafter to become due, by reason of the claims already liquidated and decided against the Mexican Republic, under the conventions between the two republics severally concluded ...

R. Del Castillo, *The Treaty of Guadalupe Hidalgo: A Legacy of Conflict* (Norman, OK: University of Oklahoma, 1990), pp. 183–99.

DOCUMENT 20   FREDERICK DOUGLASS ON THE MEXICAN WAR, 1848

Frederick Douglass, an escaped slave, became the most influential black abolitionist in America. Like most abolitionists and others opposed to the extension of slave territory, he believed the Mexican War was fundamentally a war to add slave territory to the US.

Peace! Peace! Peace!

The shout is on every lip, and emblazoned on every paper. The joyful news is told in every quarter with enthusiastic delight. We are such an exception to the great mass of our fellow countrymen in respect to everything else, and have been so accustomed to hear them rejoice over the most barbarous outrages committed upon an unoffending people, that we find it difficult to unite with them in their general exultation at this time; and for this reason, we believe that by *peace* they mean *plunder*.

In our judgment, those who have all along been loudly in favor of a vigorous prosecution of the war, and heralding its bloody triumphs with apparent rapture, and glorifying the atrocious deeds of barbarous heroism on the part of the wicked men engaged in it, have no sincere love of peace, and are not now rejoicing over *peace* but *plunder*. They have succeeded in robbing Mexico of her territory, and are rejoicing over their success under the hypocritical pretense of a regard for peace. Had they not succeeded in robbing Mexico of the most important and most valuable part of her territory, many of those now loudest in their professions of favor for peace would be loudest and wildest for war – war to the knife.

Our soul is sick of such hypocrisy. We presume the churches of Rochester will return thanks to God for peace they did nothing to bring about, and boast it as a triumph of Christianity! That an end is put to the wholesale murder in Mexico is truly just cause for rejoicing; but we are not the people to rejoice; we ought rather blush and hang our heads for shame, and, in the spirit of profound humility, crave pardon for our crimes at the hands of a God whose mercy endureth forever.

Selected Readings on Great Issues in American History, 1620–1968 (Encyclopaedia Britannica Educational Corporation, 1969), pp. D27–D28, citing Douglass's editorial in his Rochester, NY *North Star*, 17 March 1848.

GLOSSARY

Articles of Confederation   The first framework of government for the United States, created by the Continental Congress during the American Revolution. It was submitted to the states in November 1777, but not ratified until 1781. Within a few years, many Americans became convinced that the government set up by the Articles was too weak to function effectively, leading to calls for the meeting that became the Constitutional Convention, which created an entirely new Constitution to be submitted to the states for ratification.

Battle of the Maps   In the aftermath of the Webster–Ashburton Treaty in 1843, political opponents in both Great Britain and the United States accused their negotiators of giving up too much territory in the treaty. In what became known as the 'Battle of the Maps,' officials in both nations resorted to maps of questionable accuracy to 'prove' that they had not given away too much land in the negotiations.

Bear Flag Revolt   A revolt against Mexican rule by residents in California during the summer of 1845. The revolutionaries proclaimed California independent and chose American army Captain John C. Frémont to direct the affairs of the Republic of California.

Centrists   A political faction in Mexico which favored a strong national government, with most power concentrated in the central government in Mexico City. They were opposed by the *Federalists*, who wanted the provinces to have a greater measure of autonomy.

Cherokee Nation v. Georgia   A case decided by the US Supreme Court in 1831. The Cherokee tribe in Georgia sued in federal court, arguing that the laws of the state of Georgia should not be applicable within Cherokee lands. In the majority opinion, Chief Justice John Marshall expressed sympathy for the Cherokee's cause, but ruled that as a 'domestic dependent nation' they lacked the standing to bring suit in federal court.

Compromise of 1850   Following the Mexican War and the Treaty of Guadalupe Hidalgo, the US faced the question of whether or not slavery would be allowed to expand into territory gained through the Mexican Cession. The Compromise of 1850 was a series of five bills that were passed by the US Congress in August and September 1850. The five basic provisions included: (1) California would be admitted as a free state; (2) the rest of the Mexican Cession would be open to slavery based on popular sovereignty; (3) a new Fugitive Slave law was included to placate southern interests; (4) in order to placate northern interests, it was made illegal to bring slaves into the District of Columbia for the purpose of selling them; (5) territorial government was set up in New Mexico Territory and Utah Territory, and the boundary between the state of Texas and the New Mexico Territory was defined.

Corps of Discovery   See Lewis and Clark Expedition.

Demarcation Line   See 'Proclamation of 1763.'

Democratic-Republicans   One of the first political parties in the United States; formed in opposition to the Federalists in the 1790s. Thomas Jefferson and James Madison were leaders around which the new party coalesced as opposition to Washington's policies began to develop. The party existed into the mid-1820s, when factionalism broke the party apart.

Democrats   Although some trace the roots of this party to the Democratic-Republicans of Jefferson's day, the modern Democratic Party in the United States emerged in the 1830s as the supporters of Andrew Jackson in his campaigns against the National Republicans. From Jackson's administration through 1856, the Democrats won every presidential election except 1840 and 1848.

East and West Florida   Under the Spanish, and under the British from 1763 to 1783, Florida was divided into two provinces, East and West Florida, with the Apalachicola River being the boundary between the two. West Florida was at times thought to extend to the Mississippi River, so it included the Gulf coast of what are now the states of Alabama and Mississippi.

Empresario   In order to encourage settlement in Texas, Spanish authorities promised large land grants to settlers who would come to reside in Texas. These settlers were called empresarios. After the Mexican Revolution, the government of Mexico continued this policy through most of the 1820s, leading to a large number of US citizens taking up residence in Texas.

Extinguishment of title   The process by which the United States, through negotiation, purchase, and threats of military action, attempted to get Indian tribes to give up title to their lands.

Federalists (Mexico)   A political faction in Mexico which favored more political power and autonomy for the provincial governments, and less power concentrated in the central government. They were opposed by the *Centrists* who wanted a strong national government.

Federalists (US)   In the United States, Federalist was originally a term signifying those who supported the adoption of the Constitution. During Washington's administration, political factions began to develop, and the supporters of Washington's administration soon came to be called Federalists, with their opponents taking the name Democratic-Republicans.

'Fifty-Four-Forty or Fight'   During the Oregon controversy, some in America called for annexing all of the Oregon Country north to 54 degrees, 40 minutes – which is the southern border of modern Alaska. The controversy was settled in the Oregon Treaty of 1846 with the boundary between the US and British Canada generally following the 48th parallel.

Filibusterers   The term originated from Dutch and Spanish terms meaning 'free booty' and 'piracy.' In the context of American expansion, filibusterers were people who went into foreign lands to try to foment rebellions or uprisings that might lead to US annexation of the territory. Spanish Florida, Mexico, and Cuba were frequent targets of American filibusterers in the early 1800s.

Five Civilized Tribes   A name given by white observers and officials to Indian tribes in the southeastern United States that had adopted many aspects of white culture.

These tribes included the Cherokee, Chickasaw, Choctaw, Creek, and Seminole. Many of the people of these tribes were moved to the Indian Territory in the 1830s and 1840s.

French and Indian War   A conflict on the frontier between British troops and colonial militia fighting against French troops and militia, with various Indian tribes fighting on both sides. The conflict centered on control of the Ohio River Valley and the Old Northwest region. It began in 1754, and was caught up in the larger conflict known as the Seven Years' War in Europe. At the end of the war in 1763, France lost all of its territories in North America, and Great Britain became the dominant power in the eastern part of the continent.

Gadsden Purchase   The land purchased from Mexico in the Gadsden Purchase Treaty in December 1853. The treaty was an attempt to clear up some border disputes resulting from a lack of precision in the definitions of the borders in the Treaty of Guadalupe Hidalgo in 1848, and to purchase from Mexico some land south of the Gila River for possible use as a transcontinental railroad route. The purchase added approximately 30,000 square miles to US territory, and was the last addition to the territory of the contiguous US.

General Order no. 20   During the Mexican War, General Winfield Scott issued General Order no. 20 in February 1847 as American troops occupied parts of central Mexico. The order outlined how Mexican nationals were to be treated, and the punishment to be inflicted on American soldiers guilty of mistreating civilians. It was significant because, for the first time, American troops were being used for the long-term occupation of foreign territory.

Indian Removal Program   Although many US presidents have pressed for land cessions that would force the Indians to move further west, the term 'Indian Removal Program' usually refers to Andrew Jackson's program outlined in the Indian Removal Act of May 1830. Under this bill, tribes in the East would be encouraged to exchange their lands for government lands west of the Mississippi. These western lands were to be guaranteed to these tribes 'forever.' Several small tribes were moved out of the Old Northwest, and the Five Civilized Tribes were moved out of the southeast under this program.

Indian Territory   Under Jackson's Indian Removal Program, many tribes were moved out of the eastern United States into a region set aside in the West known as the Indian Territory. It was west of the borders of the states of Missouri and Arkansas, and extended from the Red River of the South to the Platte River in present-day Nebraska. It included much of what is present-day Oklahoma, Kansas, and the southern portion of Nebraska.

Joint occupancy   In the Convention of 1818, the United States and Great Britain agreed that in the Oregon Country west of the Rocky Mountains, citizens of both nations would be allowed to jointly occupy the region. This continued until the settlement of the border issue in the Oregon Treaty of 1846.

Lewis and Clark Expedition   An expedition to explore the Upper Missouri and the Pacific Northwest, launched under the direction of President Thomas Jefferson. Much of the land the party explored was part of the Louisiana Purchase, but the expedition was being planned even before the purchase was completed. The expedition was formally known as the Corps of Discovery and was led by Captain Meriwether Lewis and Captain William Clark. Leaving St Louis in May 1804 the expedition went up the Missouri, across the Rocky Mountains, and down the Columbia River and its tributaries, reaching the Pacific Coast in November 1805. They returned to St Louis in September 1806, having traveled approximately 8,000 miles in about 28 months.

Louisiana Purchase   The territory purchased by the US from France in 1803. The purchase resulted from Jefferson's desire to control the ability of US shipping to use the Mississippi River. American representatives were to offer to purchase New Orleans, but were surprised by an offer by the French to sell all of Louisiana for $15,000,000. A treaty authorizing the purchase was negotiated in the spring of 1803. The exact boundaries of the purchase were imprecise, but it is generally cited as approximately 827,000 square miles, which increased the territory of the US by about 140 per cent.

Manifest Destiny   The belief that the US was destined to expand across the North American continent, and that this destiny was evident or 'manifest.' Historians still debate the extent to which this belief was shared by the American people in the early 1800s, or whether it was a concept invented by those promoting expansion to try to attract support to their ideas.

Mexican Cession   The land that the United States annexed from Mexico as a result of the Mexican War and the Treaty of Guadalupe Hidalgo in 1848, which formally ended that war. Mexico ceded an area of 851,590 square miles, which became the states of New Mexico, Arizona, California, and parts of Texas.

Missouri Compromise   When Missouri applied for statehood as a slave state in 1819, its admission would have disrupted the balance of free and slave states, which stood at 11 each at that time. Besides the balance issue, there was concern that Missouri was so far north that it seemed to be in an area that should be kept free of slavery. In a compromise worked out in 1820, Maine was created as a new free state, and Missouri was allowed to enter the Union as a slave state. Outside of Missouri, slavery would be prohibited in the rest of the Louisiana Purchase north of 36° 30′.

Monroe Doctrine   A statement by President James Monroe in 1824 warning European nations to stay out of Western Hemisphere affairs. Primarily the work of Secretary of State John Quincy Adams, the statement was intended to discourage Russia from attempts to establish a colony in the Pacific Northwest, and to stop European nations from intervening in Latin America to try to restore Spanish rule in any of the newly independent Latin American nations.

Nootka Convention   An agreement which resulted from an affair in the Nootka Sound region in the Pacific Northwest in which a Spanish naval force had captured and imprisoned British fur traders. After intense disputes that threatened to escalate into a general war in Europe, Spain backed down and agreed to the Nootka Convention, giving up any claims to exclusive sovereignty of the northern Pacific Coast of North America.

Northwest Confederacy   A loose confederacy of several Indian tribes in the Old Northwest that fought to block US expansion into their lands in the 1790s.

Northwest Ordinances   Legislation passed by Congress during the Articles of Confederation government in 1785 and 1787 for the territorial organization of the lands north and west of the Ohio River. The ordinances outlined the procedure for territories becoming new states, and how federal lands would be surveyed in preparation for sale. An important provision of the 1787 ordinance was a provision that new states would be equal in all respects to the original 13 states.

Old Northwest   Before the Louisiana Purchase, when the Mississippi River was the western border of the United States, the lands between the Ohio River and the Mississippi River were referred to as the Northwest. Today historians refer to the region as the Old Northwest to avoid confusion with the Pacific Northwest.

Old Southwest   Similar to the *Old Northwest*, above, the lands between the Appalachian Mountains and the Mississippi River were often referred to as the Southwest before the time of the Louisiana Purchase. Today historians use the term Old Southwest to avoid confusion with the lands of the Mexican Cession in the far southwestern US.

Popular sovereignty   The political doctrine or concept that the issue of slavery in new territories of the United States should be left to the settlers in these territories. In the Compromise of 1850, the New Mexico Territory (which included what is now Arizona) was open to slavery on the basis of popular sovereignty. The territories of Kansas and Nebraska were also open to slavery on this basis by the terms of the Kansas–Nebraska Act of 1854.

Pre-emption   Legislation passed by the US Congress in 1830 and 1841 provided that settlers who had staked claims on land before it was legally available for sale had the right to purchase the land when it did officially go on sale.

Proclamation of 1763   A proclamation by the British Crown that forbade settlement by white colonists past the Demarcation Line, which generally followed the crest of the Appalachian Mountains. The Crown wished to avoid troubles with the Indians in the west over lands, but American colonists bitterly resented the proclamation.

Puros   Reformers in Mexico who wanted a 'purer' democracy in Mexico. Toward the end of the Mexican War, some members of this faction sought to make Winfield Scott a dictator in Mexico, believing that this would eventually lead to more democratic reforms.

Rectangular survey   Under the terms of the Land Ordinance of 1785, lands in the Old Northwest were to be surveyed into sections of 640 acres (a square mile) and townships of 36 sections. Most of the American lands west of the Appalachians, except for some of the former Spanish and French lands, were surveyed using this system.

Republic of Texas   When Texas settlers declared their independence from Mexico in 1836, they formed the Republic of Texas. From the time they achieved independence until the annexation of Texas into the US in 1845, the Republic of Texas was a separate, independent nation.

Republicans   The modern Republican Party was formed in 1854 in meetings in Jackson, Michigan. It quickly became a major force in the Old Northwest and, by 1860, throughout the north. Former northern Democrats, Whigs, and members of the Free Soil Party joined the new party. In 1856, their first presidential candidate, John C. Frémont, lost but made a good showing for a new party. In 1860, Abraham Lincoln became the first Republican elected to the Presidency.

The Republicans firmly opposed the expansion of slavery into new territories, and the Kansas–Nebraska controversy helped bring the party into being. Although the official position of the Republican Party was not abolitionist, southerners feared its stance on the slavery issue.

Right of deposit   In the Pinckney Treaty of 1795, Spain granted American shippers the 'right of deposit' which was the privilege of storing goods in New Orleans to await shipment out of that port. Revocation of this right by Spanish authorities in 1802, just before the region reverted to French control, led to US efforts to purchase New Orleans, which culminated in the Louisiana Purchase.

Sooners   See Squatters.

Squatters   Pioneers who settled on lands before they were officially open for sale by government land offices. Also referred to as 'sooners,' since they were on the lands 'sooner' than they should have been.

Stokes Commission   A commission chaired by Montfort Stokes, Senator from North Carolina, sent in 1835 to negotiate with the indigenous Indians in the Indian Territory, to achieve agreements to allow the US government to re-settle Indians from the East into the Indian Territory.

Tejanos   Native Mexican settlers in the Province of Texas.

West Point   The site of the US Military Academy, established in 1802. Originally the school focused primarily on military engineering, but by the time of the Mexican War it had contributed significantly to the professionalization of the officer corps of the US Army.

Whigs   A major political party in the US, active from 1834 to 1854. The party originated primarily in opposition to the policies of Andrew Jackson. The party supported several reform issues, and spending federal funds on internal improvements. Since the Whigs had significant strength in both the North and the South, the party tried to avoid partisan strife over the slavery issue. Two Whig presidents were elected to office – William Henry Harrison in 1844 and Zachary Taylor in1848 – but both died after short terms in office. In the 1850s, the renewal of the sectional crisis and the birth of the Republican Party spelt the end of the Whigs.

Wilmot Proviso   An amendment introduced to a military appropriations bill in August 1846 by Congressman David Wilmot of Pennsylvania. If passed, it would have provided that no lands taken from Mexico in the Mexican War could be open for slavery. The proviso was never passed by both houses of Congress, but debate over the issue stirred up the sectional issue throughout the war.

Worcester v. Georgia   A case decided by the US Supreme Court in 1832. Samuel Worcester was a missionary among the Cherokee who was arrested for violating a Georgia state law requiring an oath of loyalty to the state for all who worked among the Indians within the state's borders. Worcester sued, arguing that the laws of the state of Georgia were not applicable within the Cherokee nation. Partially reversing *Cherokee Nation v. Georgia*, Chief Justice John Marshall ruled that the laws of Georgia did not apply within Cherokee lands. This should have restored some measure of justice to the treatment of the Cherokee, but the federal government under President Jackson did not press to see the ruling enforced.

Adams, John (1735–1826) American statesman and patriot leader from Massachusetts during the American Revolution; member of the Continental Congress; member of the committee which drafted the Declaration of Independence; envoy to the peace conference that produced the Treaty of Paris of 1783, which ended the American Revolution. US Minister to Great Britain, 1785–1788. First vice-president of the United States, 1789–97; President of the United States, 1797–1801.

Adams, John Quincy (1767–1848) American diplomat and politician; son of President John Adams. A lawyer and statesman from Massachusetts, he served as minister to the Netherlands and later to Germany, Russia, and Great Britain. Head of the American delegation that negotiated the Treaty of Ghent, ending the War of 1812. As Secretary of State under President James Monroe, Adams negotiated the Convention of 1818 and the Adams–Onís Treaty of 1819, and was the chief architect of the Monroe Doctrine. He was elected president to succeed Monroe, but after being a brilliant Secretary of State, he proved to be a mediocre president in his 1825–9 term. Adams served as a representative from Massachusetts in the US House of Representatives from 1831 to 1848, the only US president to ever serve in the House after being president.

Ashburton See Baring, Alexander; first Lord Ashburton.

Astor, John Jacob (1763–1848) Fur trade entrepreneur and philanthropist. Founded the American Fur Company in 1808; made lucrative fur dealings in the China trade, 1800–17. His trading post in the Oregon country, Astoria, was captured by the British during the War of 1812 but restored to US control in accordance with terms of the treaty ending that war. In later years, Astor invested in New York real estate and founded the Astor Library, which in combination with other collections was consolidated to form the New York Public Library in 1895.

Austin, Moses (1761–1821) American frontiersman and Texas *empresario*. Austin was active in lead mining in southwestern Virginia and then in southeastern Missouri. In 1820, he traveled to Spanish Texas and received permission to bring 300 American families to settle in Texas. However, he died before he could fulfill this plan, and his son Stephen Austin worked to carry out the operation.

Austin, Stephen (1793–1836) Sometimes called the 'father of Texas,' he carried out plans that his father had set in motion to settle American families in Spanish (and later Mexican) Texas. Served in the Missouri territorial legislature, 1814–20. After the death of his father, he traveled to Texas and selected the area between the Brazos and Colorado rivers for the settlement of the families to be brought in from the US. In 1833 Austin went to Mexico City to present the grievances of Texas settlers to the Mexican government. He was accused of treason and imprisoned for a time. Upon returning to Texas, he became a leader in the revolution against Mexican control of Texas. In 1835–6, he was a commissioner sent by the Republic of Texas to try to obtain aid from the US. In 1836, he was defeated by Sam Houston in the election for the president of the Republic of Texas. He served briefly as secretary of state for the Republic of Texas until his death.

Baring, Alexander; first Lord Ashburton (1774–1848)   A member of the prominent British banking family that eventually became Baring Brothers. Instrumental in pioneering British investment in US trade in the early nineteenth century. Elevated to the peerage in 1835. President of the British Board of Trade during the first prime ministry of Sir Robert Peel, 1834–5. British commissioner in the negotiation of the Webster–Ashburton Treaty, 1843.

Calhoun, John C. (1782–1850)   South Carolina statesman, strong advocate of the states' rights position and Southern sectionalism generally. Elected to the US House of Representatives in 1810, he quickly became identified with the 'War Hawks' calling for war with Great Britain. Secretary of war under President James Monroe, 1817–24; elected vice-president under President John Quincy Adams in 1824, and elected vice-president again under Andrew Jackson in 1828. The Nullification Crisis with South Carolina eventually caused a split between Calhoun and Jackson, and he resigned the vice-presidency in 1832. Served briefly as secretary of state under President John Tyler, 1844–5; was elected to the Senate in 1845, where he served until his death.

Charbonneau, Toussaint (1758?–1843?)   Trader and interpreter among the Indians of the Upper Missouri. Little is known about his early life, but in October 1804 he met the Lewis and Clark expedition at the Mandan villages in present-day North Dakota. He and his wife Sacajawea accompanied Lewis and Clark to the Pacific and back to the Mandan Villages in 1806. From 1811 to 1838, Charbonneau was intermittently employed as a translator by Indian agents at the upper Missouri Indian Agency. From 1838 to his death, he worked with a number of fur trading ventures in the upper Missouri region.

Clark, William (1770–1838)   US military officer, explorer, and Indian affairs official. Co-leader of the Lewis and Clark expedition. Clark was born in the region of Virginia that was home to both Meriwether Lewis and Thomas Jefferson. He served in the Kentucky Militia for a time and then joined the US Army, where he made the acquaintance of Lewis. In 1803, Lewis asked Clark to accompany him in the Corps of Discovery (or Lewis and Clark Expedition) to explore the Upper Missouri and northwest regions. The expedition traveled up the Missouri River, across the Rockies, to the Pacific Coast and back to St Louis, 1804–6. As part of his reward for service in the expedition, Clark was made a brigadier general in the US Army. He served as the Superintendent of Indian Affairs for the Central Superintendency, headquartered in St Louis, from 1807 until his death, and was territorial governor of Missouri, 1813–20.

Clay, Henry (1777–1852)   Kentucky statesman and presidential contender. Elected to the US House of Representatives in 1810, where he soon became Speaker of the House. One of the leaders of the 'War Hawks' pressing for war with Great Britain. Campaigned for president in 1824, but when the election was thrown into the House of Representatives, he backed John Quincy Adams, and when

Adams was elected, Clay was made secretary of state. In 1831, Clay was elected to the US Senate from Kentucky. He ran unsuccessfully for the presidency again in 1832, losing to Andrew Jackson. He made a third unsuccessful bid for the presidency in 1840 as candidate of the Whig Party, but was defeated by Democrat James K. Polk. Clay was often called the 'Great Compromiser' because of his role in putting together compromises such as the one ending the 1832 Nullification Crisis with South Carolina, the Missouri Compromise in 1820, and the Compromise of 1850.

Cook, Captain James (1728–79) British naval officer and explorer. His explorations of the Pacific Northwest Coast in 1759 and 1763 helped establish a British claim to the Oregon Country. He also explored widely throughout the Pacific in three voyages, 1768–71, 1772–5, and 1776–9.

Douglas, Stephen (1813–61) Born in Vermont but became active in politics after moving to Illinois. Elected to the US Senate in 1847. With Henry Clay, he was one of the major framers of the Compromise of 1850. Because of strong interest in Illinois for a transcontinental railroad, Douglas introduced the Kansas–Nebraska Act, to set up territorial government in these regions, making them ready for statehood. The question of 'popular sovereignty' re-ignited the sectional controversy as a result of the passage of the Kansas–Nebraska Act. Ran for re-election to the Senate in 1858 and met his opponent Abraham Lincoln in a series of famous debates. Douglas won re-election, but the debates made Lincoln a national figure. Douglas was one of several candidates for president in 1860, and won the support of many Democrats, although southern Democrats broke rank with the party and nominated another candidate. He lost the 1860 presidential election to Abraham Lincoln.

Frémont, John C. (1813–90) US Army officer and western explorer. Became an officer in the US Topographical Corps, and conducted several expeditions exploring the western parts of North America. During the Mexican War, he helped to secure California under the control of US forces. However, he was court-martialed because of charges of insubordination to superior officers. He resigned from the army and settled in California. In 1856, he became the Republican Party's first presidential candidate, and made a strong showing although he lost to Democratic candidate James Buchanan. During the Civil War, he served as a major general in charge of the Department of the West, with headquarters in St Louis, MO. Political troubles there caused Lincoln to move him to a new command in Virginia. After suffering set backs there, Frémont refused to served under General Pope and resigned his commission. His later years were spent in railroad promotion and other private business ventures.

Gadsden, James (1788–1858) American railroad promoter and diplomat. He served in the US Army in the War of 1812, and in the Seminole War in Florida. As a railroad promoter, he was appointed by President Franklin Pierce to negotiate the purchase of territory from Mexico for a possible southern transcontinental railroad route. These negotiations resulted in the Gadsden Purchase in 1853.

Gray, Robert (1755–1806) US naval captain and explorer. He served in the Continental navy during the American Revolution. Headed the first US expedition to circumnavigate the world, 1787–90. During this expedition, he explored parts of the Pacific Coast. In a later voyage (1792), he sailed into the mouth of the Columbia River, naming that river for his flagship, and Gray's Harbor after himself. His explorations helped to lay the basis for a US claim to the Oregon Country. In his later years, he captained merchant ships along the Atlantic seacoast, and died at sea in the summer of 1806.

Hamilton, Alexander (1755–1804)   US military officer and statesman. Served as an artillery officer in the early months of the American Revolution; promoted to Lieutenant Colonel he served as Washington's private secretary and aide-de-camp, 1777–81. After the war, he practiced law in New York City. He was a member of both the Annapolis Convention and the Constitutional Convention, and was one of the authors of *The Federalist Papers*, urging ratification of the Constitution. Secretary of the Treasury in Washington's administration, 1789–95. In his later years he practiced law and was an active leader of the Federalist Party in New York. In July 1804 he was fatally shot by Aaron Burr in a duel and died the following day.

Herrera, José Joaquin de (1792–1854)   President of Mexico, 1844–5 and 1848–51. He rose to power in the aftermath of the failure of Santa Anna's second presidential administration. Herrera preferred to reach a negotiated settlement with the US over border issues, but ultraconservatives within Mexico brought down his administration. He was elected president again after the end of the war, but his administration was faced with many difficulties brought on by insurrections by tribal peoples, political chaos within Mexico, and economic woes.

Harrison, William Henry (1773–1841)   US military officer and politician. Born in Virginia, but his fame rests mostly on his exploits on the western frontier. Joined the US Army in 1791 and fought against Indians in the Northwest Territory. Became the territorial secretary for the Northwest Territory, and then the territorial delegate to Congress. From 1800 to 1812 he served as the territorial governor and pursued a series of treaties with Indian tribes that opened much of what is now Michigan, Indiana and Illinois for white settlement. In 1811, Harrison led the attack on Tecumseh's settlement at Prophetstown, and in the War of 1812 Harrison led the victorious American troops at the Battle of the Thames in Ontario, where Tecumseh was killed. After the War of 1812, he served in the US House. The Anti-Mason Whigs nominated him for president in 1836. In 1840, he was the candidate of the main body of the Whig party, and won the presidency. However, he died within one month of taking office, and thus has the shortest tenure of any American president.

Houston, Sam (1793–1863)   Soldier and one of the leaders of the Texas Revolution. Houston served in the US Army in the War of 1812; after the war he studied law and became a lawyer in Nashville, Tenn. Member of the US House of Representatives, 1823–7; governor of Tennessee, 1827–9. He settled in Texas in 1833; with the outbreak of the Texas Revolution, he became the head of the army of the Republic of Texas. President of the Republic of Texas, 1836–8 and again 1841–4. He successfully worked to gain annexation of Texas by the US. After Texas was admitted to the Union, he served as one of its first senators in the US Senate, 1846–59. He was elected governor of Texas in 1859, but when the Civil War began, he opposed secession and was deposed from office.

Jackson, Andrew (1767–1845)   American politician and military leader. Although born in South Carolina, he moved to Tennessee and began a law practice in 1787. He was elected to the US House from Tennessee in 1796 and to the US Senate in 1797. Financial troubles forced him to resign from the Senate, and he went home to Tennessee to become a justice in the state Supreme Court, 1798–1804. He gained national notoriety fighting Indians on the frontier and with his defeat of British forces at New Orleans in the War of 1812. After serving as Governor of the Florida Territory, 1821, and in the US Senate again, 1823–5, Jackson was elected president in 1828, the first president from a state west of the original 13 states. As president, he signed the Indian Removal Bill and oversaw the relocation of many of the Indians in the eastern US into the region beyond the Mississippi.

Jay, John (1745–1829)   American jurist, statesman and diplomat. A delegate to both the First and Second Continental Congresses, 1774 and 1775; chief justice of the New York Supreme Court, 1777; president of the Continental Congress, 1778; a member of the American delegation that negotiated the Treaty of Paris, 1783. Secretary of foreign affairs for the Congress established under the Articles of Confederation, 1784–90; collaborated with James Madison and Alexander Hamilton in writing *The Federalist Papers*, a collection of articles urging ratification of the US Constitution. After the adoption of the US Constitution, Jay served as the first chief justice of the US Supreme Court, 1789–95. In 1794, he negotiated the Jay Treaty with Great Britain. Governor of New York, 1795–1801.

Jefferson, Thomas (1743–1826)   Virginia patriot leader during the American Revolution; member of the Continental Congress; principal author of the Declaration of Independence; governor of Virginia, 1779–81; US minister to France, 1784–9. Second vice-president of the United States, 1797–1801; president of the United States, 1801–9. During his first presidential term, his administration secured the Louisiana Purchase, which increased the size of the United States by 140 percent.

Kearny, Stephen (1794–1848)   US Army officer. Served in the War of 1812, and for the next thirty years in a variety of military outposts in the West. During the Mexican War, he helped to secure New Mexico and California under US control. After California was occupied, he went to Vera Cruz in Mexico, where he commanded US troops there until an attack of yellow fever ended his career.

Knox, Henry (1750–1806)   American military officer and secretary of war in Washington's administration. Joined the American colonial army in 1775, and served as an artillery officer throughout the American Revolution. As secretary of war during the government of the Articles of Confederation, and later in the same position in President Washington's cabinet, 1785–94, he was instrumental in the formulation of much of the US government's policy toward the American Indians.

Lewis, Meriwether (1774–1809)   American military officer and explorer. Served in the US Army, 1794–1800. Private secretary to President Thomas Jefferson, 1801–3; co-leader of the Lewis and Clark Expedition, 1804–6, which explored the upper Missouri region and the Pacific Northwest. Governor of the Louisiana Territory, 1807–9. Lewis died under suspicious circumstances in 1809 along the Natchez Trace in Tennessee; it is generally believed he committed suicide, although some scholars argue that he was murdered.

Lincoln, Abraham (1809–65)   American politician. Entering politics in the late 1840s as a Whig, in the 1850s Lincoln became an important leader in the new Republican Party. Served in the Illinois State Legislature, 1834; Member of US House of Representatives, 1847–9; as a Whig Congressman, he was critical of the Mexican War and Polk's role in instigating it. Defeated by Stephen Douglas in a campaign for the US Senate, 1858. President of the United States, 1861–5. The first US president to be assassinated, Lincoln was shot on 14 April 1865 and died the following morning.

Livingston, Robert (1747–1813)   American politician and diplomat. Member of the Continental Congress from New York, 1776–83; delegate to the New York ratifying convention for the US Constitution, 1788; US minister to the court of Napoleon, 1801–5. Along with James Monroe, Livingston negotiated the Louisiana Purchase from France in 1803.

Madison, James (1751–1836)   American politician and statesman. Member of the Continental Congress, 1780–3; Member of the Virginia Legislature, 1784–6. Madison was a member of the Constitutional Convention (1787) and is regarded as the main architect of the form of government that emerged from that body. Member of the US House of Representatives from Virginia, 1789–97; US secretary of state under President Jefferson, 1801–9; president of the United States 1809–17.

Marshall, John (1755–1835)   American jurist. Served as an officer in the American Revolution, 1776–9. Began practice of law in Virginia, 1783; delegate to the Virginia ratifying convention for the US Constitution; secretary of state under President John Adams, 1800–1; chief justice of the US Supreme Court, 1801–35. Writing most of the majority opinions himself during his term as chief justice, Marshall made the Court a strong entity and firmly established the prestige of the Court.

Monroe, James (1758–1831)   American politician and statesman. Member of the Continental Congress, 1783–6; US Senator from Virginia, 1790–4; minister to France, 1794–6; governor of Virginia, 1799–1802. In 1803, President Jefferson sent Monroe to France to negotiate a purchase of New Orleans; these negotiations led to the Louisiana Purchase. He continued as a minister to France and England, 1803–7. He became secretary of state under President James Madison, 1811–17. President of the United States, 1817–25. As president, Monroe enunciated the Monroe Doctrine, warning European nations that further colonization in the Western Hemisphere would not be tolerated, and promising that the US would stay out of European affairs.

Pike, Zebulon (1779–1813)   US Army officer and explorer. As a lieutenant, he was commissioned in 1805 to take an exploring expedition into the upper regions of the Louisiana Purchase, and to find the source of the Mississippi River; he did not find the true source of the river but did establish a military outpost at Ft Snelling in what is now Minnesota. In a second expedition in 1806–7, he explored parts of Colorado and New Mexico; Pike's Peak in Colorado is named after him. During the War of 1812, he was promoted to brigadier general, and was killed in the explosion of a powder magazine during the assault on York, Ontario.

Pinckney, Thomas (1750–1828)   American statesman and diplomat. Served as an officer in the Continental Army during the American Revolution; governor of

South Carolina, 1787–9; US minister to Great Britain, 1791–6. Federalist candidate for vice-president in 1796 but was defeated by Thomas Jefferson. Member of the US House of Representatives from South Carolina, 1797–1801. While US minister to Great Britain, Pinckney went to Madrid to negotiate a treaty with Spain over US use of the Mississippi River and the 'right of deposit' for American shippers in Spanish New Orleans. The resulting treaty, known as the Pinckney Treaty or the Treaty of San Lorenzo, gave Americans free use of the Mississippi and granted the right of deposit for three years. Served as a major general in the US Army in the War of 1812.

Poinsett, Joel (1779–1851)   American politician and diplomat. Born in South Carolina. He entered diplomatic service in 1810, serving as a special agent to Rio De Plata and Chile. Secretary of state under Martin Van Buren, 1837–41. He served as a special emissary to Mexico in 1821 and 1822, and was appointed the first US minister to Mexico in 1825. The Mexican government accused him of interfering with internal Mexican politics and requested his recall in 1829.

Polk, James Knox (1795–1849)   American politician. Served in the Tennessee House of Representatives, 1823–5; member of US House of Representatives from Tennessee, 1825–39; speaker of the US House of Representatives, 1835–9; governor of Tennessee, 1839–41; president of the United States, 1845–9. During his presidency, the Oregon Treaty and the war with Mexico brought vast new territories in the West into the American domain, earning Polk the informal title of 'The Expansionist' president.

Quitman, John A. (1798–1858)   US Army officer, statesman, and filibusterer. Quitman established a law practice in Natchez, MS in the early 1820s and was elected to the Mississippi State House in 1827 and the state Senate in 1834. In 1836, he went to fight with the army of the Republic of Texas during the Texas Revolution. He served in the US Army during the Mexican War, achieving the brevet rank of major general. In 1854 he was involved in a filibustering expedition to Cuba; he was tried in connection with this for violation of the Neutrality Act, but was acquitted by a sympathetic jury. He was elected to the US House of Representatives from Mississippi in 1855, and served there until his death.

Sacajawea (c. 1786–1812?)   Shoshone Indian woman; wife of fur trader Toussaint Charbonneau, she accompanied the Lewis and Clark Expedition from the Mandan Villages westward. She had apparently been captured by Hidatsa tribesmen, and later married to Charbonneau. As she traveled with the Lewis and Clark Expedition, her presence convinced many Indians of the peacefulness of the expedition, and her reunion with her relatives among the Shoshone helped to ensure good relations with that tribe. There is conflicting evidence about the date of her death.

Santa Anna, Antonio Lopez de (1794–1876)   Mexican military leader, politician, and dictator. The son of a minor colonial official in the Spanish government, Santa Anna quickly rose to prominence in the Mexican Army during the war of Mexican independence. He supported Agustín de Iturbide in the war against the Spanish, but then helped depose Iturbide after he had claimed imperial powers. In 1829, Santa Anna helped defend Mexico from reconquest by Spain, and became a national hero. He was elected president in 1833, and remained in that office until he was captured by Texan forces at the Battle of San Jacinto in April, 1836. In 1839, he seized power as dictator, but was driven from power in 1845. During the Mexican War, the US helped Santa Anna return to Mexico from exile, hoping that he would work for peace. Instead, he took command of the forces fighting against the US. At the end of the Mexican War, he left Mexico, settling first in Jamaica and later in New Granada. Two years before his death, poor and infirm, he was allowed to return to Mexico.

Scott, Winfield (1786–1866)   US Army officer and politician. In the War of 1812, Scott achieved the rank of brigadier general, serving valiantly in battles that brought him a national reputation. He later served in Indian conflicts in the Old Northwest and the southeast. In June 1841, he became general-in-chief of the US Army. In the Mexican War, he commanded the amphibious assault on Vera Cruz and the march of the US Army to Mexico City. In 1852, he ran as the Whig candidate for president but was defeated by the Democrat Franklin Pierce. Despite his southern background, when the Civil War came he remained loyal to the union and was commanding general of the US Army during the early stages of that war. However, because of his advanced age, he retired from the army on 1 November 1861.

Slidell, John L. (1793–1871)   Diplomat for the US and later for the Confederate States of America during the Civil War. Maritime lawyer. Member of US House of Representatives from Louisiana, 1843–5. He was sent by President Polk to Mexico in 1845 to try to negotiate a purchase of territory and settle boundary disputes. US senator from Louisiana, 1853–61. During the Civil War, the seizure by Union naval forces of Slidell and a fellow diplomat from a British ship the *Trent* provoked a crisis in British–US relations that became known as the Trent Affair.

Talleyrand-Perigord, Charles Maurice de (1754–1838)   French statesman and diplomat. As a bishop in the Roman Catholic Church, he served as a representative of the clergy in the estates-general during the French Revolution. In 1797, he became foreign minister of France. When Napoleon ascended to the office of First Consul, Talleyrand was named Grand Chamberlain. As foreign minister, he negotiated the sale of the Louisiana Territory to the United States in 1803. At the end of the Napoleonic era, Talleyrand was an important figure at the Congress of Vienna.

Taylor, Zachary (1784–1850)   US Army officer and politician. Taylor joined the US Army in 1808. He served in the War of 1812, the Black Hawk War with the Sac and Fox Indians in Illinois and Wisconsin, and the Seminole War in Florida. In 1847, he was sent to the Rio Grande region to defend territory that was in dispute between the US and Mexico. Attacks on his unit there precipitated the US declaration of war on Mexico. Taylor, along with Winfield Scott, emerged as one of the major military heroes from the Mexican War. Building on this reputation Taylor entered politics, and was elected for president on the Whig ticket in 1848. In office, he worked for the admission of California as a free state and to settle other issues resulting from the Mexican War. He died in office in July 1850.

Tecumseh (1768–1813)   American Indian statesman and warrior. A chief of the Shawnee tribe, Tecumseh sought to unite all the Indians of the Old Northwest into a confederacy to block white encroachment into their lands. Throughout the

1790s and early 1800s, he was involved in many of the skirmishes between whites and Indians on the Northwest frontier. In November 1811, many of his followers were killed in an attack on their chief settlement, Prophetstown, led by the governor of the Indiana Territory, William Henry Harrison. Tecumseh was not present at that battle but was in the southeast trying to recruit other Indians to his confederacy. When the War of 1812 broke out, Tecumseh and his followers supported the British and continued fighting against the Americans. He was killed at the Battle of the Thames, in Ontario, in October 1813.

Thomas, Philemon (1763–1847) American military officer and politician. Served in the Continental Army in the American Revolution; member of the Kentucky State Legislature, 1796–9; member of the Kentucky Senate, 1800–3; moved to Louisiana in 1806. In 1810 he led an uprising against Spanish control of West Florida, and took Baton Rouge from the Spanish, leading President Madison to annex West Florida. Promoted to major general in the Louisiana militia, and served in that capacity during the War of 1812; member of US House of Representatives from Louisiana, 1831–5.

Trist, Nicholas P. (1800–74) American diplomat and statesman. He attended the US Military Academy at West Point, then studied law under Thomas Jefferson. He served as a private secretary to President Andrew Jackson. Served as chief US consul in Havana, Cuba, 1833–41. In 1847, he was sent to Mexico to try to negotiate an end to the Mexican War. In the fall of that year, he was recalled by President Polk. However, Trist, believing negotiations to be nearing a successful conclusion and encouraged by other diplomats in Mexico City, decided to remain on station and complete the negotiations, which led to the Treaty of Guadalupe Hidalgo. Faced with a completed treaty, Polk supported it but still held Trist in disrepute for his refusal to obey the recall.

Tyler, John (1790–1862) American politician. Member of Virginia House of Delegates, 1811–16; member of US House of Representatives, 1816–21; Virginia state legislator, 1823–5; governor of Virginia, 1825–6; US senator, 1827–36; vice-president, 1841, succeeding to the presidency when President Harrison died within a month of taking office; president of the US, 1841–5. Member of Confederate States Congress, 1861–2.

Van Buren, Martin (1782–1862) American politician. New York state senator, 1813–15; New York attorney-general, 1815–19; US senator from New York, 1821–9; governor of New York, 1829; secretary of state under President Andrew Jackson, 1829–31; minister to England, 1831; vice-president of the United States during Jackson's second term, 1832–7, and succeeded Jackson as president, 1837–41. In Jackson's administration and as president himself, Van Buren sought to quiet sectional tensions by opposing the annexation of Texas.

Vancouver, George (1757–98) British naval officer and explorer. A member of Captain James Cook's second and third expeditions exploring the Pacific, Vancouver was sent to explore the Pacific Northwest coast in 1791. On this and a subsequent exploration of the region, he helped to lay a claim for the British to the Oregon Country.

Washington, George (1732–99) American military officer and statesman. A Virginia planter, Washington was involved in many militia actions and in Virginia politics during the colonial era. In 1754, he led a column of Virginia militia to Ft

Necessity in the Ohio country to warn the French away from the area; however, he was forced to surrender his command in an incident that helped sparked the beginning of the French and Indian War. During the Revolutionary Era, he was a delegate to both the First and Second Continental Congresses in 1774 and 1775. In June 1775 he was chosen to command the Continental Army during the War of Independence. After the War, he presided over the Constitutional Convention in 1787 and was unanimously elected the first president of the US in 1789. After two terms, he retired from office in 1797.

Wayne, Anthony (1745–96) American military officer. He served with distinction in the American Revolution, where his bravery and impetuosity earned him the nickname 'Mad Anthony Wayne.' In 1792, President Washington sent Wayne to replace Gen. Arthur St Clair in leading troops against the Indians of the Northwest Confederacy. His defeat of the Indians at the Battle of Fallen Timbers (August 1794) near present-day Toledo, Ohio and the subsequent Treaty of Greenville (August 1795) opened large areas of southeastern Ohio to white settlement.

Webster, Daniel (1782–1852) New England politician, statesman and orator. Member of US House of Representatives from New Hampshire, 1813–17. He later moved his law practice to Boston, and served as US Senator from Massachusetts, 1827–41. As secretary of state under William Henry Harrison, Webster was the only cabinet member who did not resign when Harrison died less than a month after his inauguration. Continuing as secretary of state under John Tyler, Webster negotiated the Webster–Ashburton treaty in 1843, dealing with US– Canadian border issues in the Maine region. After finishing that treaty he resigned the secretary of state position, and re-entered the Senate. Like most Whig politicians, he was critical of the Mexican War and Polk's handling of it. He served as secretary of state under President Millard Fillmore from 1850 until his death in 1852.

Wilmot, David (1814–68) American politician and jurist. Admitted to the bar in Pennsylvania in 1834. Elected to US House of Representatives from Pennsylvania in 1845 and served until 1851. In 1846, he introduced the 'Wilmot Proviso,' an amendment to an army appropriations bill that would have banned slavery in any territory acquired from Mexico. The proviso passed the House twice but never passed the Senate; its chief significance was in keeping the issue of the expansion of slavery in the forefront of political disputes during the Mexican War. Federal judge in the 13th Judicial District, 1851–61. In 1854, Wilmot was instrumental in the founding of the Republican Party; unsuccessful Republican candidate for governor of Pennsylvania, 1857; elected to US Senate from Pennsylvania in 1860; served 1861–3. Appointed to the US Court of Claims by Abraham Lincoln in 1863; he served in that position until his death.

BIBLIOGRAPHY

ARTICLES

Eisenhower, J. (1986) 'Polk and His Generals,' in D. Richmond (ed.), *Essays on the Mexican War*. College Station, TX: Texas A&M University Press.

Horsman, R. (1961) 'American Indian Policy in the Old Northwest, 1783–1812,' *William and Mary Quarterly*, 3rd series, 18:1 (January), pp. 35–53.

Johannsen, R. (1997) 'Introduction,' pp. 3–6, and 'The Meaning of Manifest Destiny,' pp. 7–20 in S. Haynes and C. Morris (eds), *Manifest Destiny and Empire: American Antebellum Expansionism*. Arlington, TX: University of Texas.

Kanazawa, M. (1996) 'Possession is Nine Points of the Law: The Political Economy of Early Public Land Disposal,' *Explorations in Economic History*, 33, pp. 227–49.

LaFeber, W. (1993) 'An Expansionist's Dilemma,' *Constitution*, 5:3 (Fall), pp. 5–12.

Resendez, A. (1999) 'National Identity on a Shifting Border: Texas and New Mexico in the Age of Transition, 1821–1848,' *Journal of American History*, 86:2 (September), pp. 668–88.

BOOKS

Adams, E. (1913) *The Power of Ideals in American History*. New Haven, CT: Yale University.

Ambrose, S. (1996) *Undaunted Courage: Meriwether Lewis, Thomas Jefferson, and the Opening of the American West*. New York, NY: Touchstone.

Bauer, K. (1974) *The Mexican War, 1846–1848*. New York, NY: Macmillan Publishing.

Billington, R. (1956) *The Far Western Frontier*. New York, NY: Harper and Row.

Boorstin, D. (1965) *The Americans: The National Experience*. New York, NY: Vintage Books.

Brack, G. (1975) *Mexico Views Manifest Destiny: An Essay on the Origins of the Mexican War*. Albuquerque, NM: University of New Mexico Press.

Christiansen, T. and Christiansen, C. (1998) *The US–Mexican War*. San Francisco, CA: Bay Books.

Cole, W. (1974) *An Interpretive History of American Foreign Relations*. Homewood, IL: The Dorsey Press.

Cunningham, N. (1987) *In Pursuit of Reason: The Life of Thomas Jefferson*. New York, NY: Ballantine Books.

Dangerfield, G. (1952) *The Era of Good Feelings*. New York, NY: Harper and Row, 1953; reprint Chicago, IL: Ivan R. Dee, 1980.

DeConde, A. (1976) *This Affair of Louisiana*. New York, NY: Charles Scribner's Sons.

DeConde, A. (1978) *A History of American Foreign Policy*, vol. I: *Growth to World Power, 1700–1914*. 3rd edn. New York, NY: Charles Scribner's Sons.

Dowd, G. (1992) *A Spirited Resistance: The North American Indian Struggle for Unity, 1745–1815.* Baltimore, MD: Johns Hopkins University Press.

Eisenhower, J. (1989) *So Far From God: The US War with Mexico, 1846–1848.* New York, NY: Anchor Books.

Fehrenbach, T. (1995) *Fire and Blood: A History of Mexico.* College Station, TX: Texas A&M University Press.

Gates, P. (1968) *History of Public Land Law Development.* Washington, DC: Public Land Law Review Commission.

Graebner, N. (1955) *Empire on the Pacific: A Study in American Continental Expansion.* New York, NY: The Ronald Press.

Grant, U. (1999) *Personal Memoirs.* New York, NY: Penguin Putnam. Originally published 1885, 1886.

Haynes, S. and Morris, C. (eds) (1997) *Manifest Destiny and Empire: American Antebellum Expansionism.* Arlington, TX: University of Texas.

Hietala, T. (1985) *Manifest Design: Anxious Aggrandizement in Late Jacksonian America.* Ithaca, NY: Cornell University Press.

Hine, R. and Farragher, J. (2000) *The American West: A New Interpretive History.* New Haven, CT: Yale University Press.

Horsman, R. (1967) *Expansion and American Indian Policy, 1783–1812.* Ann Arbor, MI: Michigan State University.

Horsman, R. (1970) *The Frontier in the Formative Years, 1783–1815.* New York, NY: Holt, Rinehart and Winston.

Horsman, R. (1981) *Race and Manifest Destiny: The Origins of American Racial Anglo-Saxonism.* Cambridge, MA: Harvard University.

Howe, J. (1973) *From the Revolution to the Age of Jackson: Innocence and Empire in the Age of Jackson.* Englewood Cliffs, NJ: Prentice-Hall.

Hughes, J. and Cain, L. (1998) *American Economic History,* 5th edn. Reading, MA: Addison-Wesley.

Johannsen, R. (1985) *To The Halls of the Montezumas: The Mexican War in the American Imagination.* New York, NY: Oxford University Press.

Jones, H. and Rakestraw, D. (1997) *Prologue to Manifest Destiny: Anglo-American Relations in the 1840s.* Wilmington, DE: Scholarly Resources.

Leckie, R. (1993) *From Sea to Shining Sea: From the War of 1812 to the Mexican War: The Saga of America's Expansion.* New York, NY: HarperCollins.

Limerick, P. (1987) *The Legacy of Conquest: The Unbroken Past of the American West.* New York, NY: W. W. Norton.

McCoy, C. (1960) *Polk and the Presidency.* Austin, TX: University of Texas.

McPherson, J. (2001) *Ordeal By Fire: The Civil War and Reconstruction,* 3rd edn. New York, NY: McGraw-Hill.

Merk, F. (1963) *Manifest Destiny and Mission in American History.* Cambridge, MA: Harvard University Press.

Merk, F. (1967) *The Oregon Question: Essays in Anglo-American Diplomacy and Politics.* Cambridge, MA: Belknap Press of Harvard University Press.

Merk, F. (1971) *Fruits of Propaganda in the Tyler Administration.* Cambridge, MA: Harvard University Press.

Miller, J. (1960) *The Federalist Era, 1789–1801.* New York, NY: Harper Torchbooks.

Morgan, E. (1956) *The Birth of the Republic, 1763–1789.* Chicago, IL: University of Chicago.

Morris, J. and Morris, R. (1996) *Encyclopedia of American History*, 7th edn. New York, NY: HarperCollins.

Morrison, M. (1997) *Slavery and the American West: The Eclipse of Manifest Destiny and the Coming of the Civil War*. Chapel Hill, NC: University of North Carolina Press.

Nash, G. *et al.* (2000) *The American People: Creating a Nation and a Society*, brief 3rd edn. New York, NY: Longman.

Nobles, G. (1997) *American Frontiers: Cultural Encounters and Continental Conquest*. New York, NY: Hill and Wang.

Owsley, F. and Smith, G. (1997) *Filibusterers and Expansionists: Jeffersonian Manifest Destiny, 1800–1821*. Tuscaloosa, AL: University of Alabama Press.

Paterson, T. and Merrill, D. (1995) *Major Problems in American Foreign Relations*, vol. I: *To 1920*, 4th edn. Lexington, MA: D. C. Heath.

Perkins, B. (1993) *The Cambridge History of American Foreign Relations*, vol. I: *The Creation of a Republican Empire, 1776–1865*. Cambridge: Cambridge University Press.

Peterson, M. (1970) *Thomas Jefferson and the New Nation: A Biography*. New York, NY: Oxford University Press.

Pletcher, D. (1973) *The Diplomacy of Annexation: Texas, Oregon and the Mexican War*. Columbia, MO: University of Missouri Press.

Potter, D. (1976) *The Impending Crisis, 1848–1861*. New York, NY: Harper Torchbooks.

Prucha, F. (1984) *The Great Father: The United States Government and the American Indian*, vol. I. Lincoln, NE: University of Nebraska.

Reichstein, A. (1989) *Rise of the Lone Star: The Making of Texas*, trans. by Jeanne R. Willson. College Station, TX: Texas A&M University.

Stephanson, A. (1995) *Manifest Destiny: American Expansion and the Empire of Right*. New York, NY: Hill and Wang.

Van Alstyne, R. (1960) *The Rising American Empire*. New York, NY: W. W. Norton.

Wexler, A. and Braun, M. (1995) *Atlas of Westward Expansion*. New York, NY: Facts on File.

Whitaker, A. (1962) *The Mississippi Question: 1795–1803: A Study in Trade, Politics and Diplomacy*. N.p: The American Historical Association, 1934; reprint, (1962) Gloucester, MA: Peter Smith.

White, R. (1991) *'It's Your Misfortune and None of My Own': A New History of the American West*. Norman, OK: University of Oklahoma Press.

GUIDE TO FURTHER READING

PRIMARY SOURCES

A good selection of primary source documents is included in each chapter in the books in the *Major Problems* series, published by Houghton-Mifflin, that deals with various aspects of American history. Texts in this series that deal with matters connected with expansionism include T. Paterson and D. Merrill, *Major Problems in American Foreign Relations*, vol. I: *To 1920*, 5th edn (New York: Houghton-Mifflin, 2001) and C. Milner, A. Butler and D. Lewis (eds), *Major Problems in the History of the American West*, 2nd edn. (New York: Houghton-Mifflin, 1997), and A. Hurtado and P. Iverson (eds), *Major Problems in American Indian History*, 2nd edn (New York: Houghton-Mifflin, 2001). John Hollitz, *Thinking Through the Past: A Critical Thinking Approach to US History*, vol. I: *To 1877*, 2nd edn (New York: Houghton-Mifflin, 2001) includes documents in each of its chapters. David Brion Davis and Steven Mintz (eds), *The Boisterous Sea of Liberty: A Documentary History of America From Discovery Through the Civil War* (New York: Oxford, 1998) is a general collection of documents covering early American history; several examples that illustrate the theme of expansionism are included. The *Annals of America* is a multi-volume collection of primary source documents available in most research libraries (Chicago: Encyclopaedia Britannica, 1969). *Manifest Destiny*, edited by Norman Graebner, is a collection of primary source documents dealing specifically with that subject (Indianapolis: Bobbs-Merrill, 1968).

DIPLOMACY AND FOREIGN POLICY

American expansionism intersected with the interests of many foreign nations, so studies of American diplomacy and foreign policy offer valuable insights on this topic. An important recent work is B. Perkins *The Cambridge History of American Foreign Relations*, vol. I: *The Creation of a Republican Empire, 1776–1865* (Cambridge: Cambridge University Press, 1993). A valuable reference work with many articles on the people involved in America's expansionary moves, and many topics related to this, is Bruce W. Jentleson and Thomas G. Paterson (eds), *Encyclopedia of US Foreign Relations* (New York: Oxford University Press, 1997).

THE CONCEPT OF MANIFEST DESTINY

Recent years have witnessed a resurgence of interest among American historians about the concept of Manifest Destiny, accompanied by new interpretations concerning its meaning and significance. A good introduction to some of the most recent scholarship on the issue are the essays in the collection edited by Sam W. Haynes and Christopher Morris, *Manifest Destiny and Empire: American*

Antebellum Expansionism (College Station, TX: Texas A&M Press, 1997). Frederick Merk's classic monograph *Manifest Destiny and Mission in American History: A Reinterpretation* is still a work to be reckoned with in this field; it was first published in 1963 and has recently been reprinted with an excellent foreword by John Mack Faragher that places the book in the context of the ongoing debate over Manifest Destiny (Cambridge, MA: Harvard University Press, 1995). Albert K. Weinberg's *Manifest Destiny: A Study of Nationalist Expansionism in American History* (Baltimore: Johns Hopkins Press, 1935) was one of the first in-depth studies of the subject and is still a valuable resource. A recent interpretive study that explores the origin of the concept of destiny in American history is Anders Stephanson's *Manifest Destiny: American Expansion and the Empire of Right* (New York, NY: Hill and Wang, 1995). Reginald Horsman has examined the role that racial attitudes played in the development of the idea of Manifest Destiny in his *Race and Manifest Destiny: The Origins of American Racial Anglo-Saxonism* (Cambridge, MA: Harvard University Press, 1981). An important revisionist study that illustrates more recent interpretive themes is Thomas R. Hietala, *Manifest Design: Anxious Aggrandizement in Late Jacksonian America* (Ithaca, NY: Cornell University Press, 1985). An important historiographical essay is D. Berge, 'Manifest Destiny and the Historians,' in M. Malone (ed.) *Historians and the American West* (Lincoln, NE: University of Nebraska Press, 1983).

EARLY AMERICAN EXPANSIONISM

Two valuable works that help to place American expansionism in the broader context of early American history are Richard W. Van Alstyne, *The Rising American Empire* (New York: W. W. Norton, 1974) and John R. Howe, *From the Revolution Through the Age of Jackson: Innocence and Empire in the Young Republic* (Englewood Cliffs, NJ: Prentice-Hall, 1973). On Indian policy in early America, a standard work is Francis Paul Prucha, *The Great Father: The United States Government and the American*, vol. I (Lincoln, NE: University of Nebraska, 1984). Reginald Horsman explores the explicit connection of Indian policy to the expansion of US territory in his *Expansion and American Indian Policy, 1783–1812* (Ann Arbor, MI: Michigan State University, 1967). F. Owsley and G. Smith, *Filibusterers and Expansionists: Jeffersonian Manifest Destiny, 1800–1821* (Tuscaloosa, AL: University of Alabama Press, 1997) is an excellent study of the expansionary policy of the earliest presidential administrations of the nineteenth century.

THE LOUISIANA PURCHASE

A. DeConde's in-depth study, *This Affair of Louisiana* (New York, NY: Charles Scribner's Sons, 1976) will probably remain the standard work on this subject for some time to come. On the Lewis and Clark Expedition, see S. Ambrose, *Undaunted Courage: Meriwether Lewis, Thomas Jefferson, and the Opening of the American West* (New York, NY: Touchstone, 1996).

THE TEXAS AND OREGON ISSUES

D. Pletcher's *The Diplomacy of Annexation: Texas, Oregon and the Mexican War* (Columbia, MO: University of Missouri Press, 1973) is an excellent in-depth study that places the Texas and Oregon issues in the context of their times, and traces the connection of these controversies to the coming of the Mexican War. An excellent study of the early development of Texas is A. Reichstein, *Rise of the Lone Star: The Making of Texas,* trans. by Jeanne R. Willson (College Station, TX: Texas A&M University, 1989). On the Oregon controversy, see F. Merk, *The Oregon Question: Essays in Anglo-American Diplomacy and Politics* (Cambridge, MA: Belknap Press of Harvard University Press, 1967). H. Jones and D. Rakestraw place the Oregon issue in the overall context of US–British relations in their *Prologue to Manifest Destiny: Anglo-American Relations in the 1840s* (Wilmington, DE: Scholarly Resources, 1997) N. Graebner forcefully argues that the desire to control ports on the Pacific Coast, for use in overseas trade with Asia, was a major factor in American expansionism in his *Empire on the Pacific: A Study in American Continental Expansion* (New York, NY: The Ronald Press, 1955).

THE MEXICAN WAR

The major recent study of the conflict between the US and Mexico is J. Eisenhower, *So Far From God: The US War with Mexico, 1846–1848* (New York, NY: Doubleday/Anchor Books, 1989). Eisenhower has also authored a study of one of the most prominent military officers in that war, *Agent of Destiny: The Life and Times of General Winfield Scott* (New York, NY: Free Press, 1997). R. Winders focuses on military aspects of the conflict in his *Mr. Polk's Army: The American Military Experience in the Mexican War* (College Station, TX: Texas A&M University Press, 1997). The experiences and contributions of the American soldier in the Mexican War are well documented in J. McCaffrey's *Army of Manifest Destiny: The American Soldier in the Mexican War, 1846–1848* (New York: New York University Press, 1991). A recent volume that was a companion to a Public Broadcasting Corporation television series on the Mexican War is T. Christiansen and C. Christiansen, *The US–Mexican War* (San Francisco, CA: Bay Books, 1998). It is especially valuable in giving more of the Mexican side of the story than is common in most English language books on the subject. Also valuable for examining Mexican public opinion in regard to the US in this era is G. Brack, *Mexico Views Manifest Destiny: An Essay on the Origins of the Mexican War* (Albuquerque, NM: University of New Mexico Press, 1975). S. Haynes covers the role of James K. Polk in the expansion of the 1840s in his *James K. Polk and the Expansionist Impulse* (New York, NY: Penguin USA, 1997). Useful for putting the Mexican War into the context of Mexican history is T. Fehrenbach, *Fire and Blood: A History of Mexico* (College Station, TX: Texas A&M University Press, 1995). How Americans have perceived and interpreted the Mexican War is aptly covered in R. Johannsen, *To the Halls of the Montezumas: The Mexican War in the American Imagination* (New York, NY: Oxford University Press, 1985).

EXPANSIONISM AND SECTIONALISM

The connection of expansionism to the sectional crisis is well documented in one of the older classics on the era leading up to the Civil War: D. Potter, *The Impending Crisis, 1848–1861* (New York: Harper Torchbooks, 1976). A recent valuable addition to this area is M. Morrison, *Slavery and the American West: The Eclipse of Manifest Destiny and the Coming of the Civil War* (Chapel Hill, NC: University of North Carolina Press, 1997). A standard history of the American Civil War which covers the connection to expansion in its early chapters is J. McPherson, *Ordeal by Fire: The Civil War and Reconstruction*, 3rd edn (New York, NY: McGraw-Hill, 2001).

THE AMERICAN WEST

Texts on the history of the American West can help to put expansionism into the context of the overall history and development of the western regions of the US. An important revisionist work is Richard White's *It's Your Misfortune and None of My Own: A New History of the American West* (Norman, OK: University of Oklahoma Press, 1991). Patricia Limerick's *The Legacy of Conquest: The Unbroken Past of the American West* (New York, NY: W. W. Norton, 1987) also stresses many of the themes of the 'New Western History.' A recent work emphasizing more traditional interpretations is R. Hine and J. Faragher, *The American West: A New Interpretive History* (New Haven, CT: Yale University Press, 2000). Also valuable are the maps and accompanying text in A. Wexler and M. Braun, *Atlas of Westward Expansion* (New York, NY: Facts on File, 1995).

INDEX

SEMINAR STUDIES IN HISTORY

General Editors: Clive Emsley & Gordon Martel

The series was founded by Patrick Richardson in 1966. Between 1980 and 1996 Roger Lockyer edited the series before handing over to Clive Emsley (Professor of History at the Open University) and Gordon Martel (Professor of International History at the University of Northern British Columbia, Canada and Senior Research Fellow at De Montfort University).

MEDIEVAL ENGLAND

The Pre-Reformation Church in England 1400–1530 (Second edition)
Christopher Harper-Bill   0 582 28989 0

Lancastrians and Yorkists: The Wars of the Roses
David R Cook   0 582 35384 X

Family and Kinship in England 1450–1800
Will Coster   0 582 35717 9

TUDOR ENGLAND

Henry VII (Third edition)
Roger Lockyer & Andrew Thrush   0 582 20912 9

Henry VIII (Second edition)
M D Palmer   0 582 35437 4

Tudor Rebellions (Fourth edition)
Anthony Fletcher & Diarmaid MacCulloch   0 582 28990 4

The Reign of Mary I (Second edition)
Robert Tittler   0 582 06107 5

Early Tudor Parliaments 1485–1558
Michael A R Graves   0 582 03497 3

The English Reformation 1530–1570
W J Sheils   0 582 35398 X

Elizabethan Parliaments 1559–1601 (Second edition)
Michael A R Graves   0 582 29196 8

England and Europe 1485–1603 (Second edition)
Susan Doran   0 582 28991 2

The Church of England 1570–1640
Andrew Foster   0 582 35574 5

STUART BRITAIN

Social Change and Continuity: England 1550–1750 (Second edition)
Barry Coward   0 582 29442 8

James I (Second edition)
S J Houston   0 582 20911 0

The English Civil War 1640–1649
Martyn Bennett   0 582 35392 0

Charles I, 1625–1640
Brian Quintrell   0 582 00354 7

The English Republic 1649–1660 (Second edition)
Toby Barnard   0 582 08003 7

Radical Puritans in England 1550–1660
R J Acheson   0 582 35515 X

The Restoration and the England of Charles II (Second edition)
John Miller   0 582 29223 9

The Glorious Revolution (Second edition)
John Miller   0 582 29222 0

EARLY MODERN EUROPE

The Renaissance (Second edition)
Alison Brown   0 582 30781 3

The Emperor Charles V
Martyn Rady   0 582 35475 7

French Renaissance Monarchy: Francis I and Henry II (Second edition)
Robert Knecht   0 582 28707 3

The Protestant Reformation in Europe
Andrew Johnston   0 582 07020 1

The French Wars of Religion 1559–1598 (Second edition)
Robert Knecht   0 582 28533 X

Phillip II
Geoffrey Woodward   0 582 07232 8

The Thirty Years' War
Peter Limm   0 582 35373 4

Louis XIV
Peter Campbell   0 582 01770 X

Spain in the Seventeenth Century
Graham Darby   0 582 07234 4

Peter the Great
William Marshall   0 582 00355 5

EUROPE 1789–1918

Britain and the French Revolution
Clive Emsley   0 582 36961 4

Revolution and Terror in France 1789–1795 (Second edition)
D G Wright   0 582 00379 2

Napoleon and Europe
D G Wright   0 582 35457 9

The Abolition of Serfdom in Russia, 1762–1907
David Moon   0 582 29486 X

Nineteenth-Century Russia: Opposition to Autocracy
Derek Offord   0 582 35767 5

The Constitutional Monarchy in France 1814–48
Pamela Pilbeam   0 582 31210 8

The 1848 Revolutions (Second edition)
Peter Jones   0 582 06106 7

The Italian Risorgimento
M Clark   0 582 00353 9

Bismarck & Germany 1862–1890 (Second edition)
D G Williamson   0 582 29321 9

Imperial Germany 1890–1918
Ian Porter, Ian Armour and Roger Lockyer   0 582 03496 5

The Dissolution of the Austro-Hungarian Empire 1867–1918 (Second edition)
John W Mason   0 582 29466 5

Second Empire and Commune: France 1848–1871 (Second edition)
William H C Smith   0 582 28705 7

France 1870–1914 (Second edition)
Robert Gildea   0 582 29221 2

The Scramble for Africa (Second edition)
M E Chamberlain   0 582 36881 2

Late Imperial Russia 1890–1917
John F Hutchinson   0 582 32721 0

The First World War
Stuart Robson   0 582 31556 5

Austria, Prussia and Germany, 1806–1871
John Breuilly   0 582 43739 3

EUROPE SINCE 1918

The Russian Revolution (Second edition)
Anthony Wood   0 582 35559 1

Lenin's Revolution: Russia, 1917–1921
David Marples   0 582 31917 X

Stalin and Stalinism (Third edition) *Martin McCauley*	0 582 50587 9
The Weimar Republic (Second edition) *John Hiden*	0 582 28706 5
The Inter-War Crisis 1919–1939 *Richard Overy*	0 582 35379 3
Fascism and the Right in Europe, 1919–1945 *Martin Blinkhorn*	0 582 07021 X
Spain's Civil War (Second edition) *Harry Browne*	0 582 28988 2
The Third Reich (Third edition) *D G Williamson*	0 582 20914 5
The Origins of the Second World War (Second edition) *R J Overy*	0 582 29085 6
The Second World War in Europe *Paul MacKenzie*	0 582 32692 3
The French at War, 1934–1944 *Nicholas Atkin*	0 582 36899 5
Anti-Semitism before the Holocaust *Albert S Lindemann*	0 582 36964 9
The Holocaust: The Third Reich and the Jews *David Engel*	0 582 32720 2
Germany from Defeat to Partition, 1945–1963 *D G Williamson*	0 582 29218 2
Britain and Europe since 1945 *Alex May*	0 582 30778 3
Eastern Europe 1945–1969: From Stalinism to Stagnation *Ben Fowkes*	0 582 32693 1
Eastern Europe since 1970 *Bülent Gökay*	0 582 32858 6
The Khrushchev Era, 1953–1964 *Martin McCauley*	0 582 27776 0
Hitler and the Rise of the Nazi Party *Frank McDonough*	0 582 50606 9
The Soviet Union Under Brezhnev *William Tompson*	0 582 32719 9

NINETEENTH-CENTURY BRITAIN

Britain before the Reform Acts: Politics and Society 1815–1832 *Eric J Evans*	0 582 00265 6

TWENTIETH-CENTURY BRITAIN

INTERNATIONAL HISTORY

The Eastern Question 1774–1923 (Second edition)
A L Macfie   0 582 29195 X

India 1885–1947: The Unmaking of an Empire
Ian Copland   0 582 38173 8

The Origins of the First World War (Second edition)
Gordon Martel   0 582 28697 2

The United States and the First World War
Jennifer D Keene   0 582 35620 2

Anti-Semitism before the Holocaust
Albert S Lindemann   0 582 36964 9

The Origins of the Cold War, 1941–1949 (Third edition)
Martin McCauley   0 582 77284 2

Russia, America and the Cold War, 1949–1991
Martin McCauley   0 582 27936 4

The Arab–Israeli Conflict
Kirsten E Schulze   0 582 31646 4

The United Nations since 1945: Peacekeeping and the Cold War
Norrie MacQueen   0 582 35673 3

Decolonisation: The British Experience since 1945
Nicholas J White   0 582 29087 2

WORLD HISTORY

China in Transformation 1900–1949
Colin Mackerras   0 582 31209 4

Japan Faces the World, 1925–1952
Mary L Hanneman   0 582 36898 7

Japan in Transformation, 1952–2000
Jeff Kingston   0 582 41875 5

China since 1949
Linda Benson   0 582 35722 5

US HISTORY

American Abolitionists
Stanley Harrold   0 582 35738 1

The American Civil War, 1861–1865
Reid Mitchell   0 582 31973 0

America in the Progressive Era, 1890–1914
Lewis L Gould   0 582 35671 7

The United States and the First World War
Jennifer D Keene   0 582 35620 2

The Truman Years, 1945–1953
Mark S Byrnes   0 582 32904 3

The Korean War
Steven Hugh Lee   0 582 31988 9

The Origins of the Vietnam War
Fredrik Logevall   0 582 31918 8

The Vietnam War
Mitchell Hall   0 582 32859 4

American Expansionism, 1783–1860
Mark S. Joy   0 582 36965 7

The United States and Europe in the Twentieth Century
David Ryan   0 582 30864 X